From the Sagebrush of New Mexico to the Glaciers of Alaska

Frank Permenter

Published by Nomad Publications NV, 2024.

Author Frank Permenter

The author asserts the moral right to be identified as the author of this work.

ISBN PRINT 979-8-9869686-2-9

Editor J. Butler Kyle www.jbutlerkyle.com

Nomad Publications NV, Wellington, NV 89444

nomadpublicationsnv@yahoo.com

Cover art designed by Heidi Thompson, Bristlecone Studios

Table of Contents

Dedication

I dedicate this book to my loving and priceless wife, Anne Beckett, who was given to me by divine intervention from God. Who is the Being that gave me the opportunity to make all these priceless memories.

Also, my deceased wife Bobbie, who was with me for forty-four years and helped make these memories.

Acknowledgement

Debbie Gamble, Bobby Gayle, and Pat Potwin

for being loving daughters.

Jan Elliott for her hours of doing things Anne and I couldn't,

and Ed for all of his rounds of golf.

Kathy Jensen for the reliable and dependable support

for medical and life bumps.

Ryan Richards for accepting me

into the annual hunting trips with his buddies.

Andy Pitt for the many fishing trips outside of our country

like Brazil, Africa, and Canada.

Jan Kyle, Editor at Nomad Publications NV,

for helping me get this book finished and published.

1931 - 1941
New Mexico – The Homestead

For those who believe life begins before birth, my life began some time before October 27, 1931, when my parents filed for a homestead high on the continental divide in western New Mexico.

My folks, Russ and Bertha Permenter, came from the Rio Grande Valley. In June 1931 they put all their possessions in a covered, iron wheeled-wagon and left for the homestead. It took a month to travel there. They averaged maybe ten miles a day, arriving in July. The grandparents people came from Texas. Dad was born in 1900, he was thirty-one when he got to the homestead. Mom was seven years younger, so she was born in 1907. They created the town called Trechado.

They took a few cows, horses, two hound dogs, and few chickens. A couple of my uncles, including Dad's brother Wes, came along to help herd the animals. They were riding horses. They pulled the wagon with a team of mules. Mom was driving the covered wagon. Can you imagine, she had three little boys, Clarence 5-years old, Delton 3-years old, and Ed 1-year old. It would be four months before I breathed my first breath. Pioneer women were very tough. Besides driving the wagon, she was the cook when not changing diapers and looking after the other three.

Besides some kind of bed, They brought blankets and quilts, things they'd made themselves. Of course dishes for cooking and all. The trunk probably carried the clothes. One change for each of us. They'd use a wood-burning Sheep herders stove, cast iron or metal, with a flat surface to cook on and heat the place. They brought it with them as well as Kerosene lamps for light. They also brought axes and some other tools. The chickens were in a crate. Breakfast was probably dried oats, biscuits and gravy. There wasn't much meat. Mom had canned vegetables and meat before starting the trip. Snap beans would have been one of them. The cows gave us milk and butter, the chickens gave us some eggs, and wild rabbits were plentiful and very good eating.

The dogs, Jerry and Walker, loved to chase cottontail rabbits. They were named Jerry and Walker because that was the type of hound they were. They would tree the cottontails and we'd go capture them and chop their head off! We'd pull the ears apart; one would be just the skin and the other an ear. One time one dog would get the ear and then the next time the other one would get the ear. They'd eat it and then they'd run get another one. When the piñon trees died they fell. The hearts would rot out of the center so the rabbits would go in there when the dogs chased them. We'd reach in and get the rabbit, pull him out and whack him on the head. Sometimes we couldn't reach far enough, so we'd just chop a hole in the log.

In later years we collected the piñon about every six or seven years when there'd be a big crop. I love those things I could eat them by the handfuls. I like them when they're still in their hard shell.

There weren't any buildings, all six of us slept in a tent. At that altitude, 7500' winter arrives in October or November.

After locating the corner markers and a location to build living quarters they dug into the ground about 2'. With maybe 4' of logs they built a short wall around the dugout and logs for a roof, then covered it with dirt. No windows, only a door. It was probably 12' by 16'. Six of us slept and lived there. But on October 27th, I started the journey of my life in this dugout.

The house was probably made out of juniper, maybe piñon. The roof had a small peak and was made of little small diameter logs laid close together. They would stuff the cracks with moss or rabbit weed and then cover it with dirt. The dirt was clay. It would get gummy and compacted. When it rains, you walk out on it, it sticks to your feet. None of the dirt sifted through too much.

FROM THE SAGEBRUSH OF NEW MEXICO TO THE GLACIERS OF ALASKA

Slab building: Dry goods store and Post Office. Rock house we lived in.

A traveling mason came through. He was by trade a traveling rock mason and he was just traveling through the country. I don't think we paid him anything but I don't know, I was too young to remember. He used every size rock you could think of and he'd just find a place to put it in there. The rock was malpaís, it's like volcanic lava rock which is light, but this rock was real heavy. It's probably came from the El Malpais mountains.

We had no well or source of water, so all our water was hauled in the iron-wheeled wagon drawn by the horses from a neighbors windmill three miles away. We hauled water from about three miles away in 55-gallon drums. We had an iron-wheeled wagon we would take to the windmill. We'd take a chunk of wood or sometimes canvas to cover the top of the barrel so it wouldn't slop out. Water was a pretty precious item. It would be Ed and I that went and got the water. Before we left there, dad had a well drilled and they got water but it was a very small amount.

We didn't have an outhouse for a long time, we just went behind the barn. In later years they built the a two-holer. They dug a pit under it, a couple hundred feet away from the house.

Then winter arrived with 3′ of snow to cover the grass the animals ate, the only feed for them. And there was no fields yet with crops of hay or anything.

The animals couldn't dig down and get any grass. The men went out with horse-drawn team and wagon and used shovels to dig up cactus and bring home. Then they'd build a fire out in the open and use a pitchfork to hold them over the fire to burn the needles off of them. The animals survived that winter, but they were just skin and bones. They wouldn't have made it if they hadn't had the prickly pear.

We never had a thermometer but it was pretty hot in the summer. And it was a bright sun because there was hardly any clouds at all. Rain was super rare.

Somehow, we all survived because God was looking after us.

There were a few homesteaders in the area, but they were two or three miles apart. Almost all the time we lived there, there were some relatives in the area. Dad's brother being one of them. None of the relatives stayed very long. We were the last ones to leave.

You had to live on it and grow something five years before you could get the deed. We had 640 acres, which was a mile square. Weeds and sage brush were removed to make way for ground to be plowed to plant fields. The wind in the spring would blow out of the west. They started farming on the western boundary and got all of the sagebrush and rabbit weed cleared out of it. It was pretty rich soul. But after we farmed it, it was loose soil. The wind would blow it east and the weeds would hang it up. The next year or two they would clear some more brush out of the way. When we left there, they had cleared it all the way to the east section. That soil over to the west was just hard pan. The wind had blown all the top soil off. It was too mountainous and rocky up where the house and corals were. It was down below that the farm was.

We had pinto beans for food and money crop. Corn for animal feed and food for us. And of course, a large garden for canning and every day food for us during the season. We ate a lot of corn and beans.

No water was thrown out, all wash water from laundry, dishes, and bathes, was given to the livestock and dogs. When our garden was planted in the spring, we used a cup of water on each plant, just enough to make them live. My folks would take the page out of Sears Roebuck catalog and make a little tent, because we put them in the ground before the frost was done. Also, the pages were used in the outdoor toilet, (not same pages).Mom did the laundry by using a scrub board. In later years, she got a Maytag washing machine that had a gasoline motor on it. She used a clothesline to dry. The clothes dried so fast because there's no humidity in the air.

They planted probably fifty or sixty acres of pinto beans. This was a cash crop as well as food. They didn't have to hand pick them, the beans were planted in a row, when the beans pods came on, they made a sled that was just on two-by-fours about a foot or so apart. They took a cross-cut saw and sharpen the side where the teeth weren't to make a blade. They fastened it on the sled.

They'd cut them off just below the vine. Somebody would take a pitchfork and pile them in a wind row. When the pods all dry, they'd haul them up to the house into the stack lot.

A guy sat on the sled. He'd grab the corn stalks and pulled them over. When he got a lap full, he laid them aside. Somebody else would come along and they'd use a green corn stalk to tie around them to make a bundle. They'd leave them there until they dried.

My friend Boone Myers' dad had a harvester. He'd go around the country and thrash everybody's beans. We'd bag them in gunny sacks and sell the ones we didn't keep to eat. The corn they would bring to the stack lot, after we pulled the ears off the stalk. Then we would shuck the kernels off the cobbs. We'd put them in this big box called a corn sheller. When you turned the corn sheller, it would knock the kernels out of the shell. We'd feed some of the corn to the chickens and the hogs.

Dad had an old model-T roadster. He took the wheels off of it, and put a grinder on the back where the transmission-differential was. Then we put the corn in that and grind our own cornmeal. There were different sized bits for different size cornmeal. Sometimes Mom would grind the beans and make bean patties.

They used a turning plow, about a foot and a half diameter, that would slash through the earth and turn it over. They also had a disk that they pulled with the horses that would chew the ground up. Then they would use a rake to level it out. They had a planter that they used to plant the corn and beans. It was all horse drawn.

Dad would sell the beans, but he also trapped in the winter time. He was a famous coyote trapper. He would skin them and leave the skin on the legs and head. He'd turned the hide side out and cleaned the meat off. Then he built a wood structure that he could put inside through their stomach and head and the sides so the hides were stretched and they would dry nicely. He'd take a comb and brush the fur. The buyers loved his hides because they were almost ready to make a coat out of. He always got top dollar for them. He got enough money to buy winter clothes and shoes for us and some food. He'd ship them off someplace through the mail Then they would send a check back.

My parents had a staple store. They had flour, cornmeal, coffee, cigarettes, sugar, tobacco, that kinds of stuff. The outside was covered with rough slab lumber. The post office was about eight miles from us. Until we got the post office at our store.

The chickens came in the mail, fifty or so at a time. Dad built a place to put them. First he dug a trench. Then he put a metal top over it and sand over that. They would build a fire down below in the trench, that would keep the chickens warm on top of the wood. It was all enclosed. In the spring, he would order the chickens, The mailman would bring them out of Quemado or maybe Fence Lake. We always managed to have enough chickens for us to have something to eat.

After they got the dry goods store, Dad would go to Albuquerque for supplies because Mom had a brother that lived there and he'd stay with him. One time we got to go with them. It was during the war. They made this little wagon out of an axle from a regular wagon then put sideboards on it. The horse pulled it. Before we went, we'd go out in the desert and collected bones from dead animals. We had that wagon piled full of bones. They sold them for dog food or something. They put the mattress on top of all the bones. Us kids rode on top of that. There were two or three of us. We camped on the Rio Grande River. When we woke up the next morning, the dew was on the new mown alfalfa and hay fields, oh that smelled so good. Every time I smell that it reminds me of then. After we got to Albuquerque, Dad bought us a package of juicy fruit gum. I still like to buy juicy fruit once in a while because it brings back memories.

Our first school was in an old trapper's log cabin. We had different teachers throughout the years. Later the county built an Adobe one-room school house, about one mile from home. All eight grades were in this one room with one teacher. After the trappers cabin. The adobe school had a plank floor. Of course it dried out and would leave a crack. We'd love crawling underneath it to get our pencils. Sometimes we'd just poke our pencils through the crack so we'd have to go get them.

We walked to school, barefooted except winter.

We always took our own lunch. We'd started school at least by age seven, sometimes six. We had to have a certain number of kids in school for the county to provide a teacher. Ed's first year, the teacher was a bad teacher, so the next year he had to be held back. He and I were the same grade all the way through high school.

The rest of the kids were born in the dugout about every two years, sister Francelle, and brothers Phillip, Leon, and Donnie.

The Brothers – Phillip, Clarence, Leon, Donnie, and Frank. Circa 2015

When mom was pregnant with Donnie, whooping cough was coming through. Her and Dad went down to Hatch, New Mexico, where her sister lived. They stayed until after Donnie was born and mumps and whooping cough was gone. My grandparents kept us kids but we didn't get along well. They were real strict and they would always tell us, "I'm going to tell your folks and they're going to spank you when you came home." So when they did come home, we wouldn't come to the house. It almost broke Mom's heart because she wanted to see us. We were afraid we'd get whipped. Mom hated that because this all happened.

Our closest neighbors were three miles away. Everyone looked after their neighbors by helping each other. Everyone was in the same boat, so to speak, poor. We bartered with extra vegetables or whatever we had. Everyone shared what they had, if someone else needed it no matter what it was. Everybody helped everybody else.

Occasionally we would get together with the neighbors, build a fire and cook things. The kids would play kick the can or something, after dark it was hide and seek.

FROM THE SAGEBRUSH OF NEW MEXICO TO THE GLACIERS OF ALASKA

Mother's dad was a preacher. They got really upset because Mom eloped with Dad when she was thirteen or fourteen. They disowned her for a number of years. They moved later to Trechado. Then my grandpa would have a church service every Sunday at the house because there was no church. He was Church of Christ, so that's what we became.

When we left, Trechado was taken off the map. Today it shows as Techado. While we lived there, they had to have ten or twelve kids in school to have a post office. When we left, there wasn't enough people to have a post office, so we took the town off the map and the school closed.

There were Indians around but none very close. They were Navajos for the most part and some Pueblos. We didn't associate with them. We would see them when we went to the big towns, Albuquerque, Gallup and Quemado, which was hardly ever. We didn't mingle with them.

Russ and Bertha Permenter

Ed, Clarence, Delton, and Frank

Francelle, baby Donnie, Phillip, Leon circa 1945

1941-1947
California – Hard Times

In 1941, when I was ten, war broke out and also the weather became arid and windy. The crops were failing, so in 1943 we loaded all we could get in an old Ford truck and moved to California. Our homestead was sold. There was a shortage of workers everywhere in California because of the war effort.

With all our possessions in the bed of the truck and the folks put the mattresses on top. This is where all us kids rode except those little ones that could fit in front. We drove at night mostly because it was so hot. I think we left in the spring so it wasn't too bad. The next year or so we went back to New Mexico before the place was sold. Delton, he didn't like California so he had already gone back to the homestead. He raised one crop by himself, but he was just a young teenager. We had just brought a tractor before we left there, so he could farm. But he didn't make any money off of it.

We worked the orchards and vineyards, The first crop was either apricot or peaches, when those were done then it was grapes. After that, it was almonds then walnuts. After the leaves all came off and after the first of the year, Dad would prune the trees. We didn't get paid very much money but there were four or five of us pooling our money. Eventually we moved into a house, but before that we just stayed in the farm camp. They were rough built but like a motel. Just barely keep the weather out. Once we rented the old house, it had a telephone, running water, and it was $15 a month. It had an indoor toilet but the water tank was up and you had to pull the chain to make it flush. Dad would never use it. He said, "You don't do this stuff in the house." He'd go out to the outhouse. All the time we lived there he never used the inside toilet. I never used the outhouse, it stunk too much.

I also worked a while on a large dairy milking cows— 3 AM to 9 AM, rest awhile before back to milking at 3 PM and home at 9 PM. They were probably thirty or forty cows. At least they had a milking machine. It wasn't piped, so we had to pour the milk into a big container and then we'd put it through a strainer. It was Ed and I who did the milking. Terrible job, I never want to do that again.

In California, I was just a teenager maybe fifteen, I got to drive the grain truck that they harvested grain into. It wasn't huge, more of a pickup. The harvester would go around and when the bin would get about full of grain, they'd motion to me and I'd drive alongside it at the same speed they were traveling. They would pipe the grain over to my truck. When it got full, I would take the grain to the elevator and dump it. Then I'd go back down and park about where they'd come by. But when they'd be coming by. But when they'd come, I'd be asleep. The guy would throw a handful of grain at me in the truck and wake me up.

At the school in California, the local kids wore pants, not bib overalls. Dad wore bibs for years, many years after he left New Mexico he still liked his overalls. So that's what we wore too. Mom quit buying them for us when we went to California, she could feel the pain we were feeling.

FROM THE SAGEBRUSH OF NEW MEXICO TO THE GLACIERS OF ALASKA

The Ross Hall Studio
Sandpoint, Idaho

Frank 1948
age 17 yrs.

1947-1952
Idaho - The Tramp Years

All of us hated California, so in 1947 my folks bought some property in Careywood, Idaho, in the panhandle west of Lake Pend Oreille.

We tried to make a living on our property raising a few cows and goats, and a little logging. Dad milked the cows and had a hand separator. They sold the cream and we drank the milk. They would butcher a cow once in a while and that's how we got the meat. Mom would can the meat. We didn't have an ice box because we were eighteen miles out of town.

The folks had three different properties in Idaho. The one down below was about 150 acres; the one up on the basin place was probably one-hundred acres. Then they had the King property which had hardly anything on it, maybe five or ten acres; then there was another piece of property above that, that was just timber. We logged that. Of course we just had horses to use to log it with. We had a crosscut saw, and we'd carry a little jug of kerosene because pretty soon the sap built up. You had to use the kerosene to clean it off. The tree would fall, then you'd trim it up, and the horses would drag it to the landing. We'd cut it into the lengths we needed them to be. To roll the logs onto the logging truck, they built a ramp with logs and made it level. They built a logging truck out of a Chevy truck they had. It was just two-wheel drive, no air brakes or anything. Delton drove the truck. It had a six-cylinder engine and there was a lot of steep ground coming down out of the mountains. Of course the brakes wouldn't even slow it down. He used the lowest gear and crept down the hill. It's a wonder the engine didn't fly apart. We sold a few loads of logs.

Finally Mom said I'm going back to California. She wanted to go back to the church. Dad said he wasn't going back down there, so he stayed in Idaho with us. She went to California, back to Escalon. Donnie lived there and Clarence. She moved in with the them. Her parents were still alive then. Dad stayed in Idaho in the house they owned.

FRANK PERMENTER

There were no jobs close to home so we had to find work a long way aways, mostly out of state, logging or construction. One job, Ed and Clarence worked at the Cabinet Gorge Dam up on the Clark Fork River in northern Idaho. Ed was there first, and when Clarence got out of the Army he went there and then me. We were clearing right-of-way for large transmission lines, and whatever else we could find.

It was in the winter and we worked swing shift. It would get like 10° below zero. My first job was running a vibrate to vibrate the cement. They had a big crane up on a cliff that would bring up a big container of cement. There was a frame built to put it in. We'd run this vibrator and it caused all the air to come out of the cement. There were steel bars it in. It was nice and warm in there because the cement had to be warm to set up. But the job got so boring. You just stood there. Sometimes it would vibrate you down into it as far as your knees, but you could climb out.

Clarence was running a jackhammer. We could look down and see him working. It looked like it could be fun. I thought, I'd like to do that. So I asked for and got transferred to the drilling crew. It paid a little bit more money. You had to wear rain gear because you drilled down, then pretty soon you had to blow all the dust and stuff out. It was mostly mud and sludge. And it'd rain down on you. It was cold. I'd left that warm place. I was young and stupid. I didn't think about the consequences.

One time Ed and I, along with several friends, had a job cutting fence posts and telephone poles. I got burned out, so my friend Kenny T. and I decided to hitch hike to Lewiston to pick cherries that summer, about one hundred-fifty miles south. It took a couple days to get down there. We were not doing much hitching, mostly hiking. So we decided to hop on a freight train and ride the rest of the way. Everything went very good riding on top of that freight car until we went through a tunnel. In those days trains used coal for fuel and we almost chocked to death from the smoke. There was just barely room enough to clear your head, so we had to lay down on top of the car. Otherwise we'd have got our head knocked off. We didn't do that but one time.

FROM THE SAGEBRUSH OF NEW MEXICO TO THE GLACIERS OF ALASKA

We got to Lewiston with no money, but we were picking cherries so we ate a lot of them. At the end of the first day's work, we drew some money, left our sleeping bags in the orchard and went to town, ate hamburgers and to a movie, then back to our sleeping bags in the orchard. Well, that night it rained. A lot. Our sleeping bags were on the plowed ground and of course we were wet, as well as our sleeping bags were wet and muddy.

Next morning we hung the sleeping bags out on a fence to dry while we continued to pick cherries. We soon decided making posts was a much better way to make money, so back to making saw dust.

We hitch hiked back north of Bonners Ferry. We went back to making cedar posts.

Ed and I got a job from the same dam company clearing trees for the right-of-way for the big steel power lines. It was 300′ across. We had to cut and burn all the trees. We did that for a summer or two.

Somewhere along the line, Dad moved up where we were clearing right of way. Clarence came up and worked a while too. Dad was almost worthless. We thought he was old but he really wasn't. But at our age we thought he was really old.

We cut the pieces of wood into manageable pieces. Dad would put them on the fire that we built out in the middle of the right-of-way. Sometimes the fire would get away from us and we'd have to fight fire. We got paid so much a foot.

Dad and I lived in a tent. That's where we started out. We had one tent that we cooked and ate in, and another one we slept in. One day we went to work. We had a little wood stove, so we put a pot of beans in water on the stove and some water in it, so they'd be done when we got home. Well, the bear came and it smelled pretty good, so he made a new door by ripping the back open. He ate the beans and crapped in the pan and that really pissed me off. So I went hunting for him.

A few days later, he came to me and I shot him. We were cooking breakfast one morning, some bacon spilled on the stove and smoke was boiling out. Pretty soon this bear comes out of the woods. I crawled over to the tent got the .30-30 and shot him. I said, "Oh good. We've got some fresh meat." But with no refrigerator, we skinned him out, and put him in a 5-gallon galvanized cream can. Then put him in the creek, but he spoiled that day anyway.

Then later, we moved on up the line into a cabin. There were about six of us living in the cabin, all wood cutters

The cedar telephone poles were 30′ maybe taller, depending on what the tree would produce. We'd get them as tall as we could, and then cut them to the links they wanted. This was red cedar. We would peel them in the woods. They would peel off really easy. It's like a banana, you start peeling and the bark would just come right off.

But there was a guy that found some rocks that looked like they had some mineral in them. I don't think we got paid for this, but we were staking mining claims all along the side of Queen Mountain. To prove up on it you had to do a certain amount of work. We had a single jack, that's a cutting bit on a piece of steel. One guy holds the steel and the other guy hits it with a sledgehammer until we got a hole a couple of feet deep. All day long. Then we'd put a stick of dynamite in it with a cap and fuse, and when we'd get done at night we'd light the fuse and get away. It would explode and break up the ground. The next day we would clean it out and start all over again.

The minerals in it was probably silver. It wasn't gold. They would have it assayed, but it wasn't that good because they never developed a major mining claim. One of the guys that worked with us was a little renegade. His name was Elmer Alfred. He was full of energy and never listened to anyone who said 'don't do that.' Later years, he was working a similar type thing staking mining claims. When the dynamite didn't go off, he went up there to see why it didn't. But it went off just as he got there.

Then there was Willie...

Willie saw some dynamite, Couldn't understand it quite, Curiosity never pays, It rained Willie for seven days.

FROM THE SAGEBRUSH OF NEW MEXICO TO THE GLACIERS OF ALASKA

(**Editor's note:** *Little Willie* rhymes are light verses including an indifferent or cheerfully inappropriate response to a gruesome act of violence. The rhymes are attributed to Harry Graham (1874-1936). The earliest was included among the *Ruthless Rhymes for Heartless Homes* published in 1898 under Graham's pen name Col. D. Streamer while he was serving in the Coldstream Guards in England.)

Clarence was back in the army at Fort Lewis, Washington, waiting to ship out to Korea, so I went there and got a job at a military supply depot. This was 1950. The job lasted about six weeks. We processed stuff for the army to go to Korea. Things like vehicles, preparing them to ship on a boat out of Seattle or Tacoma. The Rainier Depot was south of Fort Lewis.

But when Clarence shipped out, I lost a place to stay and with two days to payday and after filling my truck with gas, I was broke. The first night I tried to sleep in the truck but didn't get much sleep. The next night I went to a flop house in Tacoma to get a bed. The manager told me I didn't want to sleep there because of drunks and thieves, but he had an extra bunk in his room, so he let me sleep there. I was so ever grateful for that. Next day I picked up my check and went back to Idaho.

I went back to Careywood near Sandpoint. I was just roaming around. Finally I went back to work at Cabinet Gorge Dam. I worked there most of that winter.

Sometimes we worked in road construction, mainly out of Montana and Washington. Jim, Francelle's husband, was a truck driver. He worked for Grant Construction so I always got a job wherever he was at because they would need somebody. Jim and I would live in a tent beside the river when we were in Montana. Then they built a road down by Walla Walla, and we stayed in a motel there. We were in high cotton.

Soon I got restless, so I went to stay with my Uncle Les in Borger, Texas. Uncle Les was married to Aunt Emma. I stayed with them. Uncle Les knew people because he'd lived there quite a while and he knew people in the oil fields. So I worked in the oil fields for six or eight months, as a 'roust about' in the natural gas wells. We did odds and ends for the drillers. When they would drill a well,

19

they would cap it. Then they would move a mile and drill another well. We would pick up the two-inch pipe that was the gas line that came from the last well they drilled. We would relay the pipe to the next well. We were assembling and un-assembling two-inch pipeline.

For a while I was a pumper's helper. The pumper was the guy who checked the horsehead well pumps. We'd just go around to make sure that everything was working like it should. Well, the pumper went on vacation, so the pumper helper became the pumper and I became the pumper's helper.

When a well would start having issues, they would fill the hole full of dry cement. They would bring out a semi-truck load of powdered cement bags. We would drag them across a table saw and split the bag open, and drop the contents in a hopper, It would go down until it got the well full. Then they would let it set up, they would take the drilling rig and drill the whole back again. They would seal it off and let it set up, then drill back through the cement. That would cure the leaks in the side of the well.

At the end of this I went back to Idaho, I was getting homesick.

Kenny came down to drive back with me, along with friend Don from Borger. We slept in the car and spent what money we had on gasoline and food. When we got to Lewiston, Idaho, we were flat broke again with three hundred miles to go and out of gas. Ken and I convinced Don to sell his coat to someone on the street. This gave us enough money to buy gas to get to Missoula,

Montana, where Ken's brother Jim worked. He gave us enough gas and food money to get home.

We probably sold the coat for about $10. It probably took about $10 to fill the tank.

Jim was a construction worker. Work in road construction in Montana. He always had money in his pocket. We got enough from him to eat a meal.

We went into a town in Montana one time and we needed gas. So we pulled into a station and it's all Indians. They're not looking at us friendly at all. I'm there to spend some money and they still don't act friendly.

FROM THE SAGEBRUSH OF NEW MEXICO TO THE GLACIERS OF ALASKA

It's like the Lone Ranger and Tonto...

The Lone Ranger and Tonto were riding around one day and all of a sudden all around them were all these Indians with feathers on them and covered in war paint. The Lone Ranger says, "Tonto what are we going to do?" Tonto looks at the Lone Rangers and says, "What do you mean <u>white man</u>!

Times were pretty tough in northern Idaho. We poached a lot of deer to eat.

1953 - 1960

Idaho to California - The Army and Married Life

It was about that time I got the motorcycle. Kenny had one, and I had one, there were some other people around there that rode with us when we did ride. We took two or three short trips with it, but didn't ride that much. Would have liked to because I really liked riding it. It was a 1951 or so Harley Davidson, a small one.

I met my first wife, Beulah, at the Grange Halls out in the country. On Saturday night they would have live music. Everybody would go there and dance. She was at one of the Grange dances. It was love right away and we got married pretty quick after that, the next spring, March 1952. Beulah was in high school. She was only sixteen and a sophomore. She had dark hair, a light brunette. Clarence was married to Helen, his war bride from Germany. They lived in Hayden Lake which is near Coeur d'Alene. They took us to Coeur d'Alene to a justice of peace, and we got married.

Ed and I traded his car for the motorcycle. He owed money on his car and I owed money on the motorcycle. From there we went to California where my parents were. We didn't have a job. There was enough equity in the car to buy a new Chevy car that was a year old. Zero miles on it.

My folks had sold all their property and moved back to California, in Escalon. Beulah and I loaded our meager things in our car and moved back to the place I did not like, but now I had a wife to support.

circa 1945

My cousins lived north of Sacramento. Since I was looking for work, they said come up to our place and look for work there. I did and found a job right away.

We settled in Sacramento, California. I went to work for Standard Oil in Davis working in a company owned gas station. They sent me to training for a week. My duties at the gas station at were filling the gas tank and being a station attendant.

After about one year, I was drafted into the US Army. I was stationed at Fort Lewis, Washington. This was January 1953. I went back to Idaho, Beulah stayed with her parents. I chose to go in the service from Sandpoint because there were about ten of us guys that went in about the same time and I didn't want to go in cold, all alone. They put us on a train to Fort Lewis. There we lost our civilian clothes and got our army haircut.

FROM THE SAGEBRUSH OF NEW MEXICO TO THE GLACIERS OF ALASKA

Everybody that was married and didn't have kids got drafted. Beulah got pregnant in time, but she had a miscarriage so I got an exemption. I had worked for Standard Oil just a short time less than the thirty-day requirement, so my medical insurance wasn't effective. The county wouldn't take us as poor people because I had a job. The bank wouldn't loan me money because I hadn't worked long enough, so Beulah couldn't have a D-and-C. She ended up not ever being able to get pregnant again. If that hadn't happened, I wouldn't have had to go in Army. No telling what would have happened after that.

I spent two years at Fort Lewis. At first I was kitchen police, which was working in the kitchen washing dishes, peeling potatoes, whatever they wanted us to do. We had 24-hours off. Then I took combat engineer training. I enjoyed the weapons training, but not the daily inspections, and restrictions.

After several month, my unit was chosen to support the training of reserves, national guard and ROTC for their annual training. I enjoyed being aggressor and ambushing them. This support was fun except doing kitchen police for them.

I enjoyed being the aggressor as the enemy. These guys were training to fight and we gave them something to fight. We would booby trap where they were going with fire crackers or something, and do all kinds of things to stop them. They were trained to keep going anyway. That was kind of fun doing that. We would pester them for a little bit and then we'd leave and go home.

One day I saw the ad on the bulletin board for a helicopter mechanic. I had a pretty high mechanical aptitude so I applied. I got selected. I liked that that was fun. We didn't have inspections and training was in Texas. We rode the train down for that. I was there four months. When I went back to Fort Lewis, I was thinking I would be transferred to the aviation section, which is what I wanted. Instead, I had to go to the motor pool and do nothing.

The training was at Gary Air Force Base near San Antonio, Texas for four months. After several weeks in the classroom, we took every piece from a Bell H-13 helicopter apart and put it back together according to the specs. It was the same model of helicopter on the TV program "Mash"

I really liked the school. I thought now I would probably get transferred to the Aviation division and away from inspections, —wrong. I was assigned to the motor pool driving a 2 ½-ton truck. Mostly hauling troops on training missions. At least I didn't have to pull guard duty and KP. This was my job for the rest of my duty time.

After I came back and was promoted and able to live off base. Beulah came up. We had an apartment in Tacoma. Then my brother Delton got killed. One Sunday, the orderly came out to where we lived and told us about it. They gave us a 30-day leave. We went back to Idaho where Ed and Clarence were. Our car was there. We went to California until after the funeral and then back to Fort Lewis.

While at Fort Lewis my brother Delton and his new wife were killed in a head on collision with a drunk driver between Spokane and Coeur d'Alene, Idaho. A very sad time.

In October, we were on maneuvers out in the field somewhere. The old man, the Commander, called me into the company tent. He offered me a transfer to the aviation section thinking I might reenlist. I said, "No, I don't want to." I was supposed to get discharged in January. My name had been submitted for a promotion to Corporal, but if I'd reenlisted my name would have got come off that list. I would rather get a discharge with a corporal rating than get to spend a little time in aviation.

The war tamed down, but I didn't have enough time to be overseas.

After my discharge we went back to Davis to my old job at Standard Oil. The rule was employers had to reinstate people back in the job they had before going into the military.

After a few months, an opportunity came up to get a Chevron station in Sacramento at Freeport and Wentworth streets. This was on the street that went to the old Sacramento airport, a very good location, but after a year and a half, the city decided to tear out all the businesses at this intersection and build a shopping center. So, we relocated to Fair Oaks about twenty miles east of Sacramento.

FROM THE SAGEBRUSH OF NEW MEXICO TO THE GLACIERS OF ALASKA

I worked on consignment, selling the inventory such as the gas, oil, and tires. Standard Oil owned the building, We stocked radiator hoses, light bulbs, and that kind of stuff. When we'd sell something, we'd buy another to replace it. It was mostly on consignment until we sold it. Then we'd pay them to get us another stock item. I didn't have money to buy much stuff, I was a consignee. I didn't hardly own anything. I did this because I was my own boss. I did hire someone because I stayed open seven days a week so I hired a high school kid to work on Sunday so I could take off.

The owner had two Mobile Oil's, which I managed for some time. When he sold it, I went down and worked in his other station for a while. About a year later my wife decided she did not need or want me anymore. That was when my divorce started. I was dissatisfied. One day I came home for lunch and there was a note to greet me, 'don't look for me,' that kind of thing. Another sad time.

I worked as an auto mechanic for a while but was too restless to stay there.

A friend who was an electrician that worked at an Air Force Base as a civilian, used to come in to the gas station to buy gas all the time. He stayed at a boarding house in Sacramento, so I moved up where he was. Then I got a job managing the gas station in Carmichael, California. This was a better paying job, I made $100 a week, but I was still unsettled after my divorce, and needed to do something else. :(

I don't mean to be offensive, but...

This guy was making love to this older lady; she was grey haired. She smiled and said, "I may have winter in my hair but I've got summer in my heart." He said, "Yeah, that's true, but if you don't get some spring in your ass we're going to be here until fall!"

FRANK PERMENTER

1960-1965
North to Alaska

Being totally fed up with California and my life, I thought about loading everything in my car (which I could) and driving east to some place I liked, find a job, and start over. One of my good friends from church, Lee D., wanted to go to Alaska but couldn't find anyone to go with him.

We hooked up and started planning the trip. I sold my car and bought a small travel trailer. Lee had a 4-wheel drive pickup. Final plans were made and we headed north in June for the three-week trip to Anchorage.

Our first stop was Gold Beach, Oregon, where Lee's brother lived. We spent a few days there fishing. Then we drove up the full length of Oregon on Highway 99 all the way to Canada. Over to Portland, and then Seattle, Washington, moving on to Bellingham, where we crossed into British Columbia at Sumas.

Here we were scrutinized by the Canadian Customs and Immigration. We had to show them all our cash and they inspected all our belongings. They wanted to make sure we would not create a problem for Canadians. We had over $1000 apiece. Of course the US Dollar went further there because the Canadian dollar was valued at less. We weren't wealthy but we were able to pay our way. This took several hours, but we weren't on any schedule.

We proceeded up through British Columbia through the Frazier River Canyon to Prince George. We reached Dawson Creek, the start of the Alcan Highway. This was a road built by the military during World War II. Since it was built to get supplies and troops to the Aleutians, where the Japanese had invaded, the road was never straight so enemy strafing could not shoot a long line of vehicles. The road was graveled, so it was very, very dusty. We had to tape around all the doors and windows to keep out a lot of the dust. Thank goodness it was not raining or it would have been very muddy and slick in places.

With Canadian fishing license, we fished any spot that looked fishy. We caught mostly trout. At Muncho Lake we rented a skiff. While Lee was tying up a fishing rig to do some trawling he was telling a story of his friend that had been doing the same thing. He tossed the rig into the lake but had neglected to tie on to his fishing line, so the lure disappeared to the bottom of the lake. We both laughed at that. Well, we had more gear, so Lee started the process over, except this time he did tie the lure to his fishing line. We ate a lot of fish on our trip.

One time we came across a mother squirrel that had been killed by a passing car. The sad part was her baby was alive. We collected him to hopefully save him. We made it a warm nest in a kitchen match box and let him ride on the truck dashboard for warmth from the defroster. Unfortunately, we didn't know what to feed him, so he passed away to squirrel heaven. Feeling sad, we decided to give it a decent burial. We made his coffin of the match box, dug a grave and placed him in the grave, covered it over with a mound of dirt and a cross with an apathy of his passing. I don't remember the words we said over him.

Thankfully we passed through Snag, Yukon in the summer. The coldest temperature ever recorded at a weather station was -84° degrees. But one thing seemed strange, I was reading a magazine at midnight without a light while Lee was driving down the road. It never got dark all night.

Another time we came around a corner in the road and saw a herd of buffalo laying down in a gravel pit. I had never heard of buffalo being this far north. We saw a few moose but not many.

The weather was good during the drive up the Alcan. We didn't have any bad weather along the way. We took a lot of pictures of the beautiful scenery. And we didn't have any problem with mosquitoes.

Anchorage

We arrived at my uncle Paul and aunt Alice's place July 10th. The family, including my cousins Patty, Penny, Tom, and Jimmy was so happy to see a relative they insisted I live with them. They had a big log house they lived in. It eventually got bulldozed over when a bank built on the lot.

It was a year or more until I convinced them I needed to get a place of my own. Which I did.

While there, I got a job as an auto mechanic until October when winter set in, but work slow so I got laid off.

Syble and the Restaurant

Across the street was a café, the Donut Hole, where I ate lunch most days. Syble worked there. In the basement was a donut bakery, so I fried donuts for a while. Then I got a job cleaning the café after closing at 10 PM. I got to know and like all the employees, and many of the customers. After closing, the cook would close the window blinds and turn on the jukebox. She had a key to the back of the jukebox so we played all the music we wanted to, dancing until everybody was ready to go home, sometimes midnight.

We were dancing in those days to Country Western music. It was the time when Porter Wagner and Buck Owens was popular. They took the 'boo hoo' out of country music and put the 'hee hee' in it.

The lady that had the café where I ate lunch and cleaned up the place was Syble Blakey. After about a year or year and a half I married her in September 1962. Syble had three daughters– Patsy 18, Bobbie Gale 14, and Debra Dawn two years old. She was divorced when she left Texas. The girls liked me a lot. Debbie was only a year old. I'm the only father she ever knew. Pat fell in love with an Air Force guy and they ended up getting married. Bobbie Gale was thirteen when we met, she was still in high school.

Frank and Syble – Anchorage, circa 1962

FROM THE SAGEBRUSH OF NEW MEXICO TO THE GLACIERS OF ALASKA

The Daughters – Debbie, Bobbie, Pat

When I finished cleaning the Donut Hole, I drove across town on the east side over by Merrill Field to Mountain View to Syble's sister and brother-in-law's other place where she worked. The restaurant stayed open all night. I got a job cleaning that one too. By the time I got through, the sun was coming up in the morning. I'd go home and sleep awhile. Uncle Paul had gone to work and Aunt Alice was doing her thing. I'd sleep, then get up and study until time to go back to the classroom. I was determined to amount to something by then.

At night I was going to college, taking classes toward an engineering degree. I'd do homework for a while until it was time to go back and fry donuts. I was taking three subjects at a time. I got my GED when I was in the Army, so I was qualified to accumulate college credits.

Syble bought the Donut Hole because of a promise from her sister and brother-in-law. They said if she'd come up from Texas and manage it for them, she would end up owning it. She renamed it Little Tex Café, since she was from Texas. There were a lot of Texans up there and they came in because of the name.

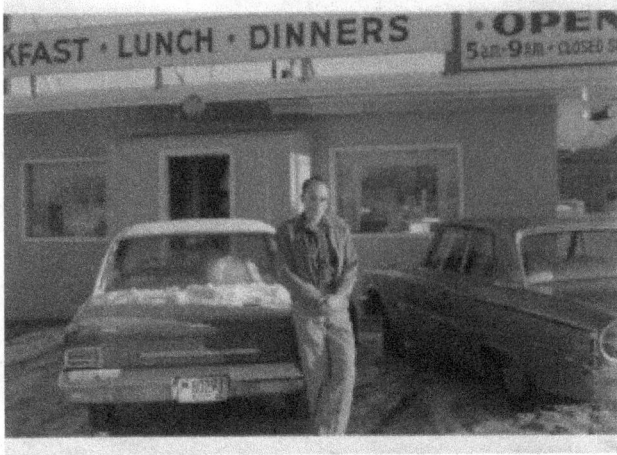

Frank in front of Little Tex Café.

There was an apartment in the basement with an outside entrance. We lived in the apartment and didn't have to pay for any electricity or utilities. It was all charged to the business. Everything we made upstairs, we got to keep. All we had to pay for was the extra help.

Springtime I secured a job with a construction contractor putting in a subdivision, including all underground utilities. The water lines had to be a minimum of 6′ deep because of permafrost. Under the roads even deeper.

After that, I worked for a land surveyor laying out lot lines.

Then they got a contract with Anchorage Gas running a profile on a gas line across Turnagain Arm. Our job was to run a profile on the existing pipeline. Kenai had a producing gas field and piped gas to Anchorage and Matanuska Valley. The area we were to run the profiles was on a large sand bar in the middle of Turnagain Arm that was 10′ under water at high tide.

Running a profile means, where the pipe is in the sand in the ground, the tide would move the covering off it and sometimes it would be laying in the bottom. It would be covered over deep with sand. We'd go out with a steel rod and stab it around until we would find the pipe. The guy with the instrument would record the depth where it was. Then we'd move a little further out and keep doing that until the tide drove us out. They wanted to know what was happening to the pipe down there, because they were putting in a second pipeline. We did that all summer.

The Kenai Peninsula had a big gas field. There was a big twelve-inch gas line that came across Turnigan Arm. Turnigan Arm is a very fierce place because of the tides. When those tides come in, they would be roaring they were making so much noise, with a wall of water in front of them. At low tide, was a sandbar in the middle. We were running profiles on the old pipeline that was there They were in the process of laying another pipeline down towards the Gulf more.

A helicopter took us out at low tide and then brought us out before high tide. The helicopter was mounted on pontoons so as not to sink in the sand. When the tide would start in, we'd hop in and go home.

One day the only helicopter available was mounted on skids, but that was okay, we had a hand-held radio. The pilot dropped us off and then went ashore, about five miles away, to wait to pick us up. This day the tide was early because of the wind and the tide changed. We could see and hear it even though it was way off in the distance.

We got on the radio and tried to call the helicopter but they couldn't hear us. When he went over to the shore, he'd sit down behind a low hill. That blocked the signal. Our radio wasn't strong enough to reach him so we started calling May Day. Merril Field, the local airport, answered and learned the situation. They relayed to the helicopter. He came and picked up two of us and then returned to get the other two.

It was just in time too, by then, the tide was maybe a few hundred feet away. There was about a size of a city block of sand left to stand on. The water was loaded with silt and very cold. They figure you'll survive about fifteen minutes when you go in the water because the water is just a few degrees above freezing. And it's so heavy with silt that you will sink because of silt-laden clothing. You would either perish from hyperthermia or sink We never took a helicopter again unless it was mounted on pontoons. That was a little scary experience.

Summertime was a great time for fishing. My uncle Paul and I flew into Kulik River, between big Kulik Lake and little Kulik Lake near Lake Iliamna, to fish for rainbow trout. We were catching fish like you can't believe. The fishing was so good we got a fish or strike with almost every cast. We stopped keeping them unless they were twenty or more inches long. It was so much fun. The people who owned the lodge owned the plane, an F 27 Fairchild. They were going over to close it down for the winter and they invited Uncle Paul to come over for free and go fish. He invited me to go with him and of course I said yes.

Frank with big catch.

Salmon had spawned earlier and many carcasses were on the river bank or in shallow water so it was easy for the Kodak brown bear to get at them to eat. Pretty soon a small cub came out of the brush and swam across the river. This alarmed the other fishermen nearby. They reeled in their lines and moved down stream because they knew the mommy was nearby looking for her baby. Being a *Cheechako*, someone new to Alaska, I believed I was ok there if I wasn't bothering the baby. A few minutes later, I heard a rustle and turned around and saw mommy on her hind legs looking over a bush towards me. I got the idea and moved downstream. We got lots of fish (the limit was ten each).

Uncle Paul and I went Arctic Grayling fishing. They were a fun fish to catch with a fly rod. We would take my little travel trailer and go to remote lakes for a few days catching them.

I always wanted to do a float trip down one of the many rivers in Alaska. The plan was to charter a float plane to drop you and your equipment off on the river of your choice, then pick you up at a certain time later at the mouth of the river. I never did get to do that because of work and lack of a fishing partner.

Bureau of Land Management office had maps that would have the profiles and everything would be in detail of each lake. I'd get a map, then hike to a remote lake to fish. The lakes were fifteen or twenty miles away, then get on a trail and walk a couple of miles. I'd go by myself which was another stupid *Cheechako* move. There's grizzly bears in Anchorage, one- or two-times people were killed by going out by themselves. The grizzlies would kill a moose or caribou and what they can't eat, they'd drag brush and dirt over it and then they go over and sleep while they digest it. If someone came close to it, they'd attack them. That's how a lot of people got killed. These were all day trips. We mostly were catching coho.

Sometimes we would drive to Homer and halibut fish. Other times charter a float plane into a remote lake where the US Forest Service had a cabin that came with a skiff you could rent. Then you could catch a lot of trout. Some of the best fishing and hunting anywhere then, not so good now.

We also did some moose and caribou hunting. A caribou is about the size of an elk but a moose produces a lot of meat. Goose hunting was good sometimes. Snowshoe rabbits were fun to hunt in the winter too. We'd shoot geese was a 12-gauge shotgun, or my bosses gun, a .30-06 for larger game. The first two moose I killed I used my boss's gun.

The first moose I shot at, the scope was fogged up and I couldn't see him, so I just kind of pointed and shot but he went away. The next time I see him, he was standing there looking at me. I shot him right under the eye and he dropped right there.

The next one was cow season, an antlerless season because they have so many moose up there. This moose was a huge cow. I could hardly carry it and I was pretty tough in those days. I had to cut it in half and quarter it so I could pack it a hundred yards or so to the car. Syble was there with me. I had a rope I tied to the moose's leg, then tied it to a tree and then the other leg to another tree so I could maneuver the carcass around.

When I got through skinning it, was all laying on the hide which I left behind. We cut chunks off and put it in this old Dodge sedan car. It was probably a thousand pounds of meat I put in the backseat and trunk. There was a lot of meat.

1963/1964 North Star Fuel

I got the job driving a fuel truck delivering heating oil. It was swing-shift; go to work at 4PM until midnight. These were good hours in summertime, but not so good in winter where 20° or 30° below zero was not uncommon. Besides the dark and cold, I had to be friendly with dogs. Some of them did not like delivery people. I only got bit a couple of times, not seriously hurt.

I just love dogs. Dogs are pretty smart. They don't want strangers on their property. If you go there, unless you're the right person. They can sense how you feel about them. Usually I see a dog and I would sit down because they don't like being looked down on, and I would talk to them. Then they'd calm down.

One time a little dog, a black cocker spaniel, was determined not to let me on the property. He met me at the gate, most of the time I could look at a dog and talk him down but this guy he wasn't having it, 'you're not coming in here, sorry.' I radioed the office and told them that no one was home and the dog was not going to let me in. They told me I would have to come back later that night when people were home.

Well, the delivery was a long way out in the country and I definitely did not want to go back. I pulled the delivery hose out. After I sprayed him with a little diesel fuel, I got into the yard to make the delivery. The dog watched me and barked until I finished my delivery. When I started back to my truck, he made another attempt to get me, he was going to get even he thought, so I washed him again with oil and got through the gate to safety. I expected to get fired over that one but the customer never called in a complaint. Most of the time I could talk to a dog and make friends but this was an exception.

Another time, I drove in this mobile home park to see where the tank was for a fuel delivery. As soon as my foot hit the ground this little black spaniel came up and bit my leg then took off. He didn't even have a chance to get acquainted. The other time I was looking for a tank, a toy Doberman Pincher was following me. He had his nose right against my leg. When I finally got back to the truck, he nipped me, just a little bit and left. 'You stick around here and I'll show you.'

Then I was delivering to a tank and there was a German Shepherd. He was on a chain about 20' long or so. He would run and hit the end of that chain and he was foaming at the mouth, barking at me but I'm out there trying to fill that tank. I had a piece of pipe about so long. I had the nozzle in one hand and I had the pipe in the other hand until I could get it done. Then I got out of there. I think if he'd ever hit the end of that chain and it broke, I was afraid of he'd have been all over me. That's what the pipe was for.

1964 Earthquake

While working for North Star Fuel, the big 1964 earthquake hit, 9.2 magnitude. It was in March and the ground was frozen down to 6' deep or more in some places. During the quake I heard loud, muffled explosions from the frozen ground breaking. There were no fires because the gas line was designed to shut down in emergencies. I had just gotten off work and stopped at a music record shop. As I entered the door, the floor started to tremble and I said, "Your furnace must be out of balance." When a plate-glass show window shattered we knew it was an earthquake.

I ran outside to get in my truck and go home. The earth was shaking so badly I had to hold on to my truck to stay erect. Someone yelled to watch the overhead wires, they were swaying back and forth. I moved out in the street and tried to stand up but it was like being on a surfboard in the waving water. The waves in the earth were made by the quake. I was at the corner of 4th and D streets, when the north side of the street started sliding down hill. I could see people on the sidewalk trying to come toward us but it was steep and icy. I watched an apartment building on the corner as the whole wall fell out and watched a dresser in the room bouncing up and down. Then a table lamp fell out of the building and then the dresser. After the quake settled down, I looked at Anchorage Western Hotel, fourteen stories high and the tallest building in town, still swaying like a whip antenna. It didn't fall down, but several other buildings did crumble.

We lived in Spenard, like a little suburb of Anchorage. The house was across a little creek. One side was Spenard, the other side was Anchorage.

Because of debris blocking the streets, I had to make several detours. When I got there, the bridge was collapsed. So I got out, waded across the creek, it was just a little stream. I ran home, about half a mile and was relieved to find all my family safe. The apartment we lived in had no heat, so we went to Uncle Paul's to spend the night. They had a propane cook stove so we had heat, a white-gas lantern for light, and a battery-operated radio.

We sat in front of the gas element listening to the radio reporters getting information to people all night long. The chandelier hanging over the table swung all that night.

Everyone was expecting a tsunami on the Kenai Peninsula. We were getting continuous reports. But it never came because we were land miles away from where the tsunami landed. Valdez and Seward were hit very bad. Valdez was relocated. This was the second time. The first time it burned down. Seward had lots of damage, even boats in trees half a mile inland. But it never hit Anchorage.

The National Guard was out all-night rescuing people and posted all over town to stop looters. They were protecting people's properties. Their houses were destroyed and they didn't want their personal possessions looted. They had portable generators for lights. Since the generators used diesel, I was given a pass and delivered fuel to them for a few days. To go in those neighborhoods to deliver fuel for their emergency generators because there was no electricity.

The destruction was almost unbelievable, it looked like everything was put in a large cement mixer and turned on. There were foundations but the rest of the houses was scattered around. Devastation was all over town. I had a black and white movie camera and took about 400' of film. There would be a foundation for a house, but there was no house on it. Because the earth jiggled from side to side, there'd be a pile of rubble over here or over there. The trees looked like they had been in a cement mixer, they were laying all directions. All the houses in what is now called Earthquake Park where all destroyed. There were lots of aftershocks.

The summer of 1965, Syble sold the café to somebody and we bought a house in Jewel Lake area. We bought a brand-new truck we picked it up in Seattle. I took leave for the summer and we had the whole summer off. We put a canopy on the truck, got some lumber and built a stand to support a mattress so we could sleep there and cut our travel expenses. There was a propane hot plate, so we did not have to eat out often either. We kind of lived out of the truck for a while. We went to Texas where Syble was from and spent the entire summer down there, the two girls, Bobbie Gale and Deborah, Syble and I. Pat was married by then.

We stopped at the Grand Canyon and Carlsbad Caverns on the way down. Went to a baseball game in the Astrodome in Houston. Swam in the Gulf of Mexico and went cat fishing. There was a big gathering with relatives to eat the cat fish and all the fresh vegetables we couldn't get in Anchorage. On the way back home to Alaska we stopped in Las Vegas and took in a show or two.

We drove to Seattle to catch the Alaska Ferry to Haines, then drive to Anchorage. The ferry stopped in several towns in Southeast Alaska, Juneau being one of them. The ferry terminal was downtown. We had a couple of hours, so we walked uptown around. It was windy and raining very hard. I said, "You couldn't pay me to live here." And guess what, a bit after we got home the company offered me a promotion to be a District Manager in Juneau. I was not real excited about living there but realized if I turned it down, they probably wouldn't ask again.

Petrolane
1965 - 1984 - The Yo-Yo Years

Then Petrolane bought out North Star Fuel. North Star Fuel owned two or three fuel companies supplying heating oil plus two or three gas propane companies. Petrolane wanted the propane companies. They incorporated it all together. I didn't really like my job, but it paid fairly well. When Petrolane bought it, we had to join the Union and we got a big increase in pay.

Soon after the sale, my new boss took me off the oil truck and put me on the propane truck. Then they moved me into the sales department. I was taking care of walk-in customers, filling small propane tanks, answering the telephone, selling stuff to people, and emptying the railcars of propane and maintaining the parts inventory. It was a job I really liked and was very happy to get off the delivery truck. I loved selling, so I fit right in.

The regional manager was also the district manager at that time, because they didn't have both. When they'd be low on something, I'd tell them they'd need more. Finally I said, "Let me do that. I know how." They gave me the job to do purchasing but the manager would sign the purchase order.

I didn't realize it at the time, but they had started training me for management. The company also got me involved in servicing propane appliances and installing them, including the gas supply system.

A gas supply system includes the tank and the regulator lines. You have to set the tank run, the line, and hook up all the appliances. If they have problems with them, you are the repairman also. They moved everyone they wanted to keep into the propane side. One morning they said they sold the company you now have a new boss. They put me where they wanted me, they saw great potential.

After a few months the company offered me a promotion as District Manager in Fairbank. I turned it down because Anchorage was too cold but not nearly as cold as Fairbanks. It got so cold in dead of winter there it was very hard to turn the steering wheel and all lubricants had to be very thin. Vehicles were inside a heated building at night. I declined, but thanked them for the offer.

1965 (August) to 1968 (February) – Juneau, a new offer with a transfer

They needed me there right away, so they flew me down for a week or ten days before consummating the deal. Back home, they gave me some more training and then back to Juneau for a new life. I was very concerned if I could do the job, but happy to give it a try. The company packed up my family and all our possessions and flew them down. Our car was shipped on a barge.

After living in a motel for a week or two I bought a new, then largest mobile home and parked it behind the office to be our new home. For the future I would not have an 8:00-to-5:00 job but the hours were from "till-to-can't." Usually, ten to twelve hours, six days-a-week. There was so much work that had not been done that should have been. It was difficult to know where to start.

The largest challenge was past due customer accounts. Sixty-six percent were past due. The previous manager would send past due notices, but many were ignored. Follow-up notices of "pay or service would be discontinued" were sent, but many of these were ignored. I started sending past due notices to most delinquent accounts with a note, "Contact me for payment arrangements by a certain date or service would discontinued." Some customers followed my request. Those accounts that still ignored it, I took them to small claims court. Some paid the amount or we came up with a plan agreeable to all for final payment. Those that did not pay, then the account was given to a collection agency. This was the very hardest thing I had ever done and lots of people did not like me for it. But I had orders to follow.

I got full support from my supervisors. After a year or so the accounts receivables were brought into an acceptable order. I think my hair started turning grey. Sales were growing even with the account problem. We were having so many the installations and service work required many long hours. It seemed I never got rested, but I was determined to accomplish the responsibility given to me. My efforts were recognized by my supervisors and it helped much down the road in my future with Petrolane Gas.

Anyway, my first-hand memories were not real good of Juneau. We not only sold propane for home and businesses for heating, we also had a pet store with complete with dozens of tropical fish, several kinds of exotic birds, monkeys, gerbils, and supplies for all of them. They had pets because every business was just trying to survive. There was no pet store so they thought they could make a few bucks doing that. I even sold RV appliances because I was willing to take customers money. The propane company wasn't creating much income, it was in the days before things started booming. It took me about a year to convince Petrolane to get rid of the pet department, much to my relief. The gal that ran the pet store, she bought everything and moved it somewhere else.

Electricity was so high, we were deluged with demands for propane gas from residences, restaurants, laundry mats, and any place that had an unusual heating requirement. Propane was delivered to Juneau by barges from Seattle in large tanks. Barge service came on a weekly basis. I got real good lessons in sales, service, and customer relations; which some I still apply in today's life. I learned how to treat people. I recognized the need for services and provided them.

Eventually everything got to a normal environment. Then after about a year and a half, Petrolane bought the propane business in Ketchikan; Queens Gas owned by Don K. and it did not come with a manager. I told my boss I wanted the job but he told me they needed me in Juneau. I told them I could do both and they said they could not afford that, because they would have to pay me more money because I wouldn't do both jobs without more money.

1968 (February) to 1970 (July) Ketchikan

Well after a week or so, my boss called and asked how I planned to do that. I convinced him I could do it. Now I had two challenges rolled into one. I spent time between both places but stayed on in Juneau until I could find and hire an assistant for there. Then Petrolane moved Syble and the girls and I to Ketchikan. I hired and trained a service man, delivery driver and office manager.

Oh, how much better this was. People were friendly, paid their bill on time, and happy to get professional service. There was much to be done besides serving customers, like changing the existing system to Petrolane's system.

The previous company had their way of doing things and Petrolane had their way of doing things. Accounting was one thing, safety was another. It was before credit cards, you had to open an account. With the old system, someone would say, 'bill me,' but Petrolane wouldn't do that. They had to fill out a credit report application. A lot of people didn't like doing that.

The House of Representatives politician was one of my biggest delinquent customers that owed money. I pulled his tank out, and he spread a lot of bad words about me. Bobbies father-in-law was in the Rotary club. He wanted me to join. I said sure. But Rotary didn't want me in because the politician was giving Petrolane a bad name. He was one of those guys that said, 'You listen to me and pay attention.' I joined anyway.

One of the guys, he was an artist and another one of my people in Ketchikan who didn't like to pay their bill, he wanted to join. They always poled the members for any objections. I didn't think he'd make a good Rotarian, I voted against him and he didn't get in.

It was challenging but interesting.

Anyway, the previous owner was a plumbing business and got into propane because of necessity to satisfy his customers. He didn't have any background in propane so much was lacking as far as knowledge of the product and safety. Another challenge for me.

Finally, we got a 1000-gallon tank the freight boat could handle. We'd send it out and they could fill their own tanks. But they'd fill it until the pumps stopped, instead of filling it to a safe level. Those kind of things. The regulator would get water on it and they'd freeze and cause fires. Propane safety was also a high priority. I held safety classes for all the camps and worked closely with the fire departments with propane related training films and demonstrations. Much of this was not new to the fire departments but a review to most of them. It was good training for those new in the department. I spent lots and lots of time, at no charge to them, to go to camps and spend a few days to a week teaching the supervisors the safe way to do things. They loved me on Prince of Wales, they thought I was God.

The economy for the most part in Ketchikan was the large pulp mill and many logging companies. I spent many trips to all the logging camps in Ketchikan area and up to Sitka, repairing cook stoves, gas dryers, and water heaters. Public electricity was not available in the camps and was very high priced in town so propane was the least expensive energy source.

They'd build a little shack or take travel trailers, and clear off a space, for example in Thorne Bay, that's where they brought all the log in to float them to the pulp mill. That's how all those villages became villages, because before that there was no one living there. Like in Thorne Bay, it'd be somebody in a float house who was a fisherman or something like that. There was about three-hundred people population. Whale Pass, Coffman Cove, Naukati, all those places, that's how they came to be. And that's how Petrolane got in on the beginning.

The logging camp workers had mobile homes to house their families. The women were very happy to get their cook stoves tuned up and thermostats calibrated, and have lots of hot water. Their propane and supplies were delivered by a supply boat on a weekly basis. Propane was delivered to them from Petrolane Gas in Ketchikan in 100# cylinders (about twenty-four gallons) which were very heavy and often ran out while taking a hot shower or eating. This was another challenge for me to get bulk delivery to their residence (more on that later).

The propane came to Ketchikan by rail barge out of Canada. A rail barge is a barge that hauls rail cars on it with rails the cars set on. They had a hookup down in Prince Rupert and they put the rail car on it there. The barge came in about once a month with supplies for the pulp mill. They had twenty or thirty rail cars on it.

As you would expect it always arrived at night.

The barge would tie up to our dock, It was my job to attach the hoses and transfer the propane to the two 20,000-gallon land storage tanks on shore. I'd have all night to pump the liquid off the railcar. This was about a four-hour job and I didn't have anyone else to change off with.

Next morning they would take off. Always at night because that's the way the barge company worked. They needed to be at another place in the morning. But that was okay, it gave me uninterrupted time to make plans for what the next challenge was.

And that challenge was to supply the logging camps with propane.

There was a freight boat that crossed to Prince of Wales once a week. It would take supplies out and bring empty propane tanks back. They'd drop off the 100-pound sized propane cylinders on our float at the plant. These held twenty-four gallons of propane and we'd fill them up. We'd have a few days to fill them. We would have thirty to seventy to fill. It would almost sink our wood-float dock. Sometimes the dock would actually be underwater. It had logs under it to keep it afloat though. When they were all done, I would drop them off on freight docks float to go back to the camps again.

I was able to get some 1,000-gallon export tanks to fill and send to the larger camps, and supplied them with pump and hoses so they could fill cylinders at the camp. This was welcome by both the camp and my employees. My next plan was to put some storage tanks at the camps and a bulk-delivery truck to fill tanks at the point-of-use at the camp. This took a lot of time and lobbying but I finally got it done. One of us in Ketchikan would go out when needed to fill the tanks. My next job was to find someone in the camp to do the deliveries on a commission basis when we were not able to do it ourselves.

1,000-gallon tanks on the landing craft.

I trained the person. We had someone over there most of the time. They were kind of laid back because they worked hard, and if they'd have a weekend off, maybe they sometimes wanted to go fishing. We supplied them with the pumps, hoses, and training.

I loved going to the logging camps because they had the best food in the mess hall, and nicely furnished bunk houses. The only way to get to and from any place in Southeastern Alaska was by float plane or boat. This was very interesting to me. My first boat was 19' for hunting and fishing. Fishing and deer hunting was as good as it gets and I really enjoyed doing that with what little spare time I had.

To hunt with a boat, you lay the anchor on the hull and have a long line go into the cove. You have another line tied to the boat so you come in at high tide. You push the anchor off into deep water, but you still have line that's tied to the boat. When the tide goes out, the boat doesn't. Well, usually. Sometimes I had to wait for the tide to back come in.

Frank camping on the beach out of Ketchikan.

On time Mom and Dad came up and we went fishing. We put the boat out, it had a lot longer run out than I thought. We had to wait two or three hours the next morning for it to float in. The Forest Service had a covered picnic table where we camped. The wind came up and it was kinda cool. We were sleeping in sleeping bags where the picnic table was. We had some blankets and quilts and stuff. I said, "Man, if we had some nails or something we could put a curtain up here." So Mom opens up her purse and hands me some nails. She'd been outside and there were some nails there and she picked them up planning to bring them in, but hadn't taken them out of her purse yet. So we had one wind break. This was mom and Dad and of course Syble and I.

In the meantime, I had to go to Juneau at least once or twice a month.

1970 (July) to April (1971) - Texas to Seattle

In July 1970, my wife Sybil developed lung cancer and was pronounced terminal. She was in Texas at the time visiting her family. I told my supervisor I had to be replaced because I had to be with my wife in Texas. He told me to go look after my wife and I was to stay on the payroll as long as was necessary. This was something that was hard to imagine. I didn't think I deserved it but they insisted, so for three months I stayed in Texas.

When Syble had completed the maximum treatments and was able to travel, we went to Seattle where she was admitted to Virginia Mason hospital. Petrolane gave me a job in the Seattle plant where I did mostly sales and dispatching.

After Syble passed away in November, Petrolane asked me to come back to Alaska but I told them I had a teenager to raise. They let me stay and work in Seattle. In March 1971, Sybil's oldest daughter Pat told me she wanted to take Debra back to Vancouver with her and for me to go back to Alaska. Bobbie Gale and her young daughter Dawn and son Robbie moved into a rental in Seattle.

I don't remember when I started smoking cigars. After I quit cigarettes in 1970, when I ended up back in Ketchikan, I started smoking a pipe. When I went to Juneau, there was a pipe tobacco store you could get all these flavors. I got acquainted with the guy who owned the store. I'd go visit with him and try different mixtures. I finally found a combination I liked. So I smoked a pipe all the time. Cigars were kind of a treat. I'd buy one once in a while, like when we'd go to Canada we'd buy Canadian Cigars because you couldn't buy them here in the States. Then I started chewing smokeless tobacco. I chewed that the longest. I could never do Copenhagen. It was too strong. It would make me sick at my stomach. I tried Skoal and it was pretty heavy too. It was made by the same people who made Copenhagen. Bobbie's brother chewed Kodiak, it had a mint flavor and I liked that. Beechnut was kind of sweet and very juicy, it was the stems off the tobacco vine.

One time, I had a professional guy put red stepping stones on the whole back lot in Yuma. We had a problem when it rained, because the rain would come down and run underneath the house. We were fixing up a way to divert the water. I took a bite of that Copenhagen and pretty soon I'd start getting really dizzy. That's when I started noticing I'd get dizzy when I put a bite in my mouth, especially if it was a very big bite. I tapered off. Quite a bit. Then I finally cut it off, because it was affecting my blood pressure. I could get two or three sessions off one cigar.

Grandma liked to dip powdered snuff. She would take a teaspoon and hold on to the spoon end and use the handle to dip the snuff. It was in a jar. She'd get some and she'd put it on her lip like that. She'd go to the kitchen wood stove and spit once. That's all she'd ever spit. You would never know she had to in her mouth.

Grandpa chewed plug tobacco. Sometimes he'd bite it off sometimes he'd cut it off. I remember he chewed Brown's mule. It had a little metal red mule with its feet stuck in the tobacco. The plug was covered in cellophane. He chewed Star tobacco too. It had a golden star out of metal. I don't think he ever spit either.

I tried pot several times but was never one to take it up as a habit. I had a dealer in Wrangle, he and his brother were my propane dealers, I'd go up there about once a year. They smoked pot. We'd go in the hot tub, drink wine and smoke pot together. I did that a time or two. Then I had a friend in Petersburg, the guy who we went into the mobile telephone business with, he smoked pot some. I only did it once or twice with him. I'd get a little bit of a high, but I could do the same thing with alcohol and I could control that. I just stuck with alcohol.

I'm not opposed to pot, I don't think it's any worse than drinking, but some people feel it's going to lead to cocaine and stuff like that. And that would be a concern, but in my mind I knew I would never become addicted to it, because I was so against the idea. The loss of control.

My drink of choice was gin and tonic for quite a bit. Margaritas taste pretty good too, if you use a lot of ice. I like vodka with orange juice or tomato juice, sometimes gin with two spoons of olive juice. When we were mining with Lowell and Suzanne, we got into gin and olives. Those big colossal olives. The four of us, we would drink a quart a night. We got pretty lit.

When we were in Brazil, I ordered a Bloody Mary. It had celery, little onions, all these vegetables and about a half a bottle of Tabasco sauce, and tomato juice. I couldn't drink it. I told them, "Take the vegetables off and I'll put the hot sauce in." Then in first class on the plane, we got free drinks. So what the heck, I want a Bloody Mary but I don't want any vegetables in it or not too hot. Probably it was just tomato juice and vodka.

If I drink more than three, I probably won't feel good tomorrow. I've never had a hangover, where I'd be sick or anything, but I just feel tired and worn out. I kind of like tequila too, on the rocks. In Algodones, they have liquor stores down there, but they don't open until 10:00 o'clock or something like that. That one year, they had samples of tequila, they have some of them that are really good. We'd buy a bottle of the good stuff. Last time I was down there, they wouldn't give me a sample of that real good tasting one.

I keep rum around for Jan. I like being a good host. Anne likes crown royal, so every Christmas I get her a big bottle. Anne she doesn't drink hardly anything but beer, except Crown Royal. She's not a lush by any means. When I drink red beer, I'll put a little bit of tomato juice in a glass and top it off with beer, then stir it up with just a little salt on top. The doctor said, "Don't sprinkle salt, don't eat it." Well dang it, I'm 93-years old, I know I'm not going to live forever, so why not enjoy it as much as you can.

Another guy walked in a bar...

This guy walked into a bar and he had on his leash a seeing eye dog. The bartender says, "Can I help you?" The guy says, "No, just looking around."

1971 to 1977 - Back to Ketchikan

In March, 1971, Petrolane wanted me back in Ketchikan as things were not going as they should. I was very happy with this change, so in April I went back to the state and work I loved.

I picked up where I left off with my original responsibilities. I was trying to get my life back together. I found a nice one-bedroom apartment on the beach with a beautiful view. I was lonely and did some dating, until I met Bobbie Elliott.

The Alaska Loggers Association, which I was heavily involved in, had a convention every year They always had a dance and a banquet. I was looking for someone to go with me. Everybody knows everybody, it's a little town. My office manager, she referred me to this one lady but she already had a date. Then she told me about Bobbie, so I contacted her. She was involved with the pulp mill and all the loggers. You know everybody's a friend in Ketchikan. We went to the banquet together, then we started chumming around. It wasn't very long that we got married after that. We met October and got married December, 29th, 1971. Bobbie had three children– Kathy lived in Portland, Oregon; Ed and Bo were still living at home.

Frank and Bobbie – Ketchikan, December 29, 1971

My top priority was establishing propane gas bulk delivery on Prince of Wales Island.

After a lot of lobbying, I got a new gas delivery truck for Ketchikan, then the Ketchikan truck was moved to Thorne Bay on POW Island, also several 1,000-gallon bulk tanks, and 100-gallon bulk tanks at homes to be filled with the bulk truck. This was all for Thorne Bay which was mostly made up of families that worked for Ketchikan Pulp Company.

The roads on Prince of Wales were mostly all gravel. When I first got there it was paved from the Hydaburg turnoff to Klawock. Then they between Craig and Klawock. Hollis was under construction for a couple of years. I hated that road. I tore up more tires on that gravel. The contractor was terrible. But it allowed us to service Hydaburg, Craig, Klawock, Coffman Cove, Naukati, and Whale Pass. Although this wouldn't happen for a year or so.

In the meantime I continued taking care of business in Ketchikan.

Coast Guard Repeaters

The Coast Guard had marine radio repeater on top of the mountains for mariners to use their marine radio from out at sea and along the coast line. This is because you're so far away, satellites are the only thing that would work or these repeaters, so they have to be close enough together. They had batteries they had to keep charged. These operated on 12-volt batteries that were recharged from thermal-electric generators that burned propane. We contracted with the Coast Guard to refill the propane tanks up on mountain tops once a year in the summer throughout Southeast and South-Central Alaska, all the way from Ketchikan to Kodiak. There were eight or ten of these throughout both regions, two in Valdez, one in Juneau, one in Petersburg, one in Wrangle, two in Ketchikan, and one on Prince of Wales.

They normally had seven or so 500-gallon tanks up there. Usually there was two full tanks when we went up but that was their reserves. We'd refill the other five 500-gallon tanks. Since all were remote, except for a couple, we had to charter and coordinate a tug and barge to take tanks to the base of the mountain, as well as a helicopter to service them.

Typical Coast Guard Repeater Site.

The helicopter would drop me off on the mountain top. My partner would have the helicopter drop him off on the barge to fill the 100-gallon tanks from the 1,000-gallon tanks on the barge. He would hook them one at a time on to the helicopter to deliver to the mountain top for me to transfer the propane to the tanks on site. The helicopter would pick up the ones I had emptied and returned them to be refilled. So this process would go on for several hours until all tanks on sight were refilled.

Flying in a string of propane tanks.

Each site was different but they all had the same equipment. The process was kind of crude because they didn't have a cement truck to pour a pad or anything for the big tanks to set on. The building had a transmitter and other radio equipment I didn't know what was. The burner was inside the shelter. The landing craft, or barge, would come out of the local harbor. They would take the landing craft with the big tanks (1000 gallon) to use to fill the little tanks (100-gallon each). Sometimes the barge didn't get close enough to the land so they could fill the tanks. That's when the big helicopter would fly the 1000-gallon tanks to the propane bulk plant, where we'd have them fill them, then fly them back to the barge.

Barge work.

There was a repeater on a High Mountain, out of Ketchikan. Of course those we could just do out of our yard. We didn't need a barge, just trucks. When we went to Petersburg, it was probably 20 miles from Petersburg, so the barge went there. When we would do the Zarembo Island which was up by Wrangel, the barge would go to the base of the mountain there. We'd ride in the helicopter up to the job. In Juneau, Robert Barron Peak was really tall. We didn't have to have a barge for that either. We could truck the propane to where they could fill the tank. The one on Prince of Wales was up by Ratz Harbor. We did that one from the end of a logging road, so of course we didn't need a barge.

Site high atop a mountain.

Many of the mountain tops were very high and clouds would some time delay our work.

The one in Valdez was on top of Montague Peak. This is the first land mass coming in from the waters of Prince William, out of the Gulf of Alaska. The moist air would come in and form clouds as soon as it hit that peak. One time we sat in Valdez seven days waiting for the clouds to clear before we could go up there. When we finally did get up there, I told the helicopter guy, because someone before us had to stay up there for a week, if the clouds come in and you can't get to us we're going to head right down the mountain this way, and pointed in that direction.

Various sites.

Well, the clouds moved in and we got down the mountain a little ways and it was shale rock. It was too steep to climb down. You couldn't stand up without sliding. We went back to the site and eventually the clouds lifted. They came up and got us. Another time when they dropped us off, the pilot was using instruments. As soon as he flew off, he disappeared back into the clouds.

Some technicians a week or two before were trapped up there for a week. No fun there.

FROM THE SAGEBRUSH OF NEW MEXICO TO THE GLACIERS OF ALASKA

There was no survival gear on any of the mountains. Looking back on it now, I would not have done what we did. I would've told them we had to have a radio so I could have direct communication with the helicopter and the barge down below. You're up there naked. We didn't have communication or anything. Then the technician told me there was a radio inside the shelter. Well we didn't know that. It might as well have been in Heaven as far as we were concerned because we wouldn't have known what it was, what we were looking at, or how to use it. We were propane people not radio technicians.

You would've thought there would have been C-rations or sleeping bags up there. Occasionally those radio technicians would spend a whole week up there because sometimes the clouds just didn't leave the peak. The last time we filled it, they had moved the site down to Naked Island which is down at a lower level so they didn't have to fight the clouds so much.

Fortunately, the Coast Guard had to pay for the tug, barge, and helicopter when we had a delay.

The other site in Valdez is just as you leave the harbor, the site up there was Halibut Peak. We could do that one from of the yard, we didn't have to use the barge. I got involved with a lot of stuff like that, that most people didn't know about.

When we did the one on Prince of Wales, we didn't use a barge. We just put the tanks on the beach and the trucks from Craig would go down and fill all the tanks. And then they would transfer them up to the mountain. This was below Hydaburg.

One time when we went to Kodiak to service Gull Point, we got to our two wives. That was a highlight for her. It was seventy miles in a helicopter from Kodiak across Shelikof Straits to a bluff above the coast. The barge hauled jet fuel for the chopper, so long distances for the helicopter was not a big issue.

Preparing to fly across Shelikof Straits.

They dropped me and Bobbie off at the mountain top. The other guy and his wife were down at the bottom to fill the little tanks. In 1912 there was a big volcanic eruption on the Alaska Peninsula and dumped about a foot of ash over all that area including Kodiak. Over the years the topsoil built up on top of the volcanic ash and made new vegetation grew. The brown Kodiak Grizzly bears would dig through the top soil down to the original roots to eat. That would leave a recess in the ground.

Bobbie would lay in one of those recesses enjoying the warm sun and read a book. Two Kodiak were grazing about half a mile away. Her job was to read her book and keep an eye on those bears if they started feeding toward us. If they did, the chopper would haze them away. They never did, but when we first got there one was near our work area and the chopper hazed him or her away and they never came back.

It was always a relief when all these sites were refueled. I was always happy to get back on solid ground. I was getting to not look forward to riding in a helicopter. It seemed each year a chopper would crash and this always bothered me. I know they generally are safe but you never know!!!!

FROM THE SAGEBRUSH OF NEW MEXICO TO THE GLACIERS OF ALASKA

When I lived in Juneau, I flew to Anchorage quite often. One direction we would stop in Cordova and on the return it would be Yakitat. That's the only time I've been in Cordova, was at the airport. We went to the Kennecott copper mine on the Copper River. It's strange, that million-dollar bridge that didn't go anywhere.

In Ketchikan, we tried to get the state or the feds to build a bridge across Tongass Narrows to the airport. There was a reason for it, Ketchikan is chiseled out of rocks, so there's no place to expand, and Gravina Island has lots of ground they could build on. We would call it A Bridge To Nowhere, but it would have been a good thing for the community.

It would have been so expensive, because of all the cruise ships going through there. They would have had to build a bridge high enough. What they would have had to do was go north where it's the higher end of the island. It would have had to be real long too. The bridge from Juneau to Douglas Island didn't have to be very high. Those narrows were pretty shallow. When the cruise ships come in to Ketchikan, the town just turns into an ant hill. When the cruise ships are gone at the end of the season, half the windows are boarded up with plywood.

1977 to 1983 - Back to Juneau

I was still an Area Manager for Southeast, Alaska, for Petrolane. With all this going on I had to go to Juneau at least once or twice a month to deal with things that wasn't getting done, things that needed my decisions on, budgets, that kind of stuff, and training people. This was in Juneau as well as Ketchikan. So we moved from Ketchikan back to Juneau. We got a 23' boat and took with us.

For the first month we rented an apartment before buying a three-bedroom duplex with a friend. A year or two later our friend was moved to Anchorage and we bought out his interest. The three-bedroom duplex was only about a half mile from Petrolane's office and plant. It was also near Thunder Mountain. In the winter time, snow whipped by the wind would build a large cornice or curl over the top of the mountain. When the curl got out far enough it would come crashing down, being unsupported, taking out trees and boulders and causing a loud crashing sound, hence "Thunder Mountain." This occurred two or three times a year.

This area where we lived was in Glacier Valley, and it joined the Juneau Glacier Ice field about sixteen miles from downtown Juneau. Our temperature was always colder than downtown

because the cold would come down from the ice field. That lowered the temperature a lot. Sometimes we would get a foot of snow and downtown would get rain. Wood smoke from stoves and fireplaces could only rise a short way off the ground because of the cold temperature layer so the smoke looked like it hit a solid ceiling. If the temperature was low enough, borough would ban wood burning of any kind.

Mendenhall Glacier about three-quarters of a mile from our house.

Because of the snow in the valley, it was wonderful cross-country skiing and snowshoeing.

Across the channel from downtown was Douglas Island. The Borough built a ski resort and it was a good place to ski, however we only did cross-country.

But the snow and cold did make a lot of problems in our work.

FROM THE SAGEBRUSH OF NEW MEXICO TO THE GLACIERS OF ALASKA

The cold air coming off the ice fields down into the valley. The first major problem I had, our truck ran on propane and the process of getting fuel to the carburetor, it came out of the tank as a liquid and went through a converter that kept it warm by circulating coolant in the engine. The radiator got low and it wasn't changing the propane to a vapor, it just iced everything up. We fought that all day, it was crazy. Finally I called my boss in Anchorage, I said, "I don't know what's going on." He said check the radiator. I did. It was low, we put water in it and everything was fine. If we had to pick up or set tanks in the snow in the valley, that was a problem. The temperature was below zero sometimes out in the valley. In town, they'd get snow sometimes but usually it stayed above freezing. But it was just another day for us.

We received our propane from Ketchikan by ocean going barge. Although we tried to coordinate shipments, sometimes we did not get them on time and we ran out of propane for the town. One time I had to charter a tug and barge out of Seattle to bring a couple of rail cars of propane. Now I knew how the Coast Guard regarded propane and other flammable liquids, so I knew notifying them would prevent me doing what I had to do. So I did it without notifying them.

When they saw the barge coming up the channel the Commander called me and asked, "What the hell is going on here!" I explained our dilemma to him and told him he would be deluged with calls from restaurants, laundry mats, and residences because they depended on propane for meals, drying clothes, and heat. He finally said, "Okay, but if I you ever try doing that again I will put you in jail!" Well fortunately we did run out again but was always able to get a regular barge shipment out of Ketchikan, not always by rail cars, but smaller vessels which had different regulations.

I never had to do it, I knew damn well if I called him he'd say, "No you gotta do this or that." They'd have made so many restrictions that I couldn't have done it. It's better to ask for forgiveness than it is to ask for permission. That was a good example.

I'd have been in trouble with the Coast Guard again if they had found out it was me.

Speaking of the Coast Guard, another time they called me and said that a rail car had broken off a rail barge in the Gulf of Alaska and was floating down the channel, and was a hazard to navigation. Since it could not be recovered, they wanted to shoot it with one of their big guns and sink it. They wanted to know how far away they needed to be to shoot it. I asked how far their gun would reach. They wanted to be closer, so BANG. But they missed, so another shot and this time they hit it.

A huge cloud of vaporized propane went into the air, but hitting it felt so good they shot it again and created a huge blevy that scorched the beard of one of the seamen. They were apparently five-hundred yards away. One of the seamen sent me pictures of the chain of events. I sent them to my supervisor in Anchorage and he enlarged one and put it on his office wall. On a future visit by the Coast Guard to his office, they wanted to know where he got that picture. Of course they never did not find out.

Bobbie and I had a close friend that ran for the House of Representatives and another as candidate for governor. We wanted to see Suzanne J. elected. They had an art studio in Juneau, Lowell was an artist. They were Republican, so we got heavily involved in politics.

The president of the 4th District Republicans resigned and I was nominated to replace him. I refused but every one vowed they would support me so I reluctantly accepted. Bobbie had previously been elected President of the women's club so we were Mr. and Mrs. Republican of Juneau. We had fundraisers and all kinds of stuff. Anybody who wanted to donate stuff would bring it to the location we chose and all the proceeds would go into the political fund.

That same year the republican for Governor was determined to move the Capital to interior Alaska. That would cause Juneau to become a ghost town because most of the State workers lived in Juneau and business depended on them to buy their goods and services. We refused to cooperate with the state. People from Washington D.C. and Anchorage they were always contacting me trying to get me to convince people to destroy our town.

FROM THE SAGEBRUSH OF NEW MEXICO TO THE GLACIERS OF ALASKA

I had to make the call to the news media of our choice to *not* support the Republican candidate for Governor. I got calls from Republicans in Washington DC and state level trying to convince Juneau to vote for the Republican candidate. I did not go out by myself until this was all over. It was terrible and I wished a thousand times I had never got involved with politics. Politics can be, and is, a dirty business. I still feel that way today and I still vote but it ends there.

Soon after, I quit Petrolane Gas because they would not raise my office manager and serviceman's pay. And I was tired of training them for them to quit to go work for the State for more money.

But, Petrolane rehired me to do a feasibility study. This lasted for about one year. My goal was to see if we could generate enough volume of propane and diesel to have our own transportation system. My mission started by calling on all the logging companies, canneries, and fish processing plants, US Forrest Service camps, and cities that generated their own electracy in Southeast and Western Alaska. I started making the calls in Southeast because it was closer to home.

After covering that area, my supervisor and I went to Western Alaska– Sand Point, King Cove, and Cold Bay. This was where the major airlines landed to refuel, about half way to end of the Aleutian Islands chain. Our next stop was Dutch Harbor. This is where the big fishing boats, including the huge crab boats, unloaded their catch to be processed. Dutch Harbor has many fish processing plants. Then on to Dillingham, Kotzebue and Nome. These places could get one maybe two barge shipments a year out of Seattle because of the ice and storms.

After we experienced bad weather and vast distances, the decision was made to scrap this project altogether. It was a very interesting project and experience for me. I would not have ever got that experience but for Petrolane Gas. So back to Juneau to find some other experience.

While in Juneau, our neighbor Chuck K. was a professional photographer, director, and producer. He sold a lot of pictures to Hollywood. Some of them were in the movie *Jaws*. He got to know a lot of the movie stars and they decided to make a movie in Juneau. It was called *The Timber Tramps*. Claude Akins., Leon Ames, Cesar Romero, Michael Hagerty and others were in it. They showed the premier in Juneau and of course we got tickets. The movie didn't amount to much and didn't go anywhere. But it was interesting to see it and of course we were invited to the premiere.

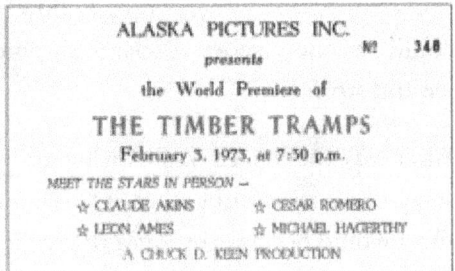

Movie premier invitations.

1983 & 1984 Mining
There's Gold In Them Thar Hills

Each summer we joined Lowell and Susanne with our RVs and spent our summer vacations camping and fishing in British Columbia. One night we were camped by Surprise Lake, near Atlin, and heard this banging and clanging coming down the rocky dirt road. Soon this couple stopped, they were on their way to get fuel barrels filled. They had a placer mine close by, so we spent a few hours visiting with them. They were in the process of building a trommel to reclaim gold. They invited us over to visit their claim the next day.

It was very interesting. Lowell and I could see where some improvements could be made. Lowell was an accomplished artist so he had a better eye than I did for that sort of thing.

Lowell and Suzanne had an art gallery. Lowell was a very good artist but that field is also slow to get going well. We have six of his paintings. Suzanne was not elected, so both of them were ready for a change.

On the ferry from Skagway to Juneau we were reminiscing our vacation and I said I would enjoy doing placer mining. Lowell said, "Are you serious?" I replied, "I am very serious." Looking back at the mess we had in politics and disappointments; I was ready for a change.

All of us agreed it was a good idea.

After I quit Petrolane Gas, I had started a small business on my own as a factory representative for construction tools and maintenance equipment. This was a very slow business to get going well and I was out of patience, so it was easy to walk away from.

Bobbie was working for the State of Alaska as finance officer for Public Safety. When Legislative Affairs advertised for a finance officer, she applied for the job and got it. It paid quite a bit more, so all was well for some time. But when it was time for budgets, she got the budget completed and then one

Friday at 5 o'clock her supervisor came into her office and gave her five minutes to clean out her desk. She was terminated with no reason. Legislative Affairs were not union so no job protection. Her being a Republican working for a Democrat-controlled situation, she was out the door. She was privy to some of the bad things the Democrats were doing and she had passed some of it on to the Republicans, so that was the reason for firing her, but they didn't have to give a reason. So, all in all she was ready for a change.

On the ferry back from Skagway to Juneau, we started making plans for a new adventure. Fist we needed a place to mine. Plans were made for Lowell and I to go back to Atlin, British Columbia, and find a person that had mining claims that we could lease, since foreigners were not allowed to own land.

We'd go look and see how other people did stuff. With Lowell being a professional artist he could picture stuff in his mind and then we'd go make it.

After that, we had to make a design and plan for our new operation. We had to make plans how to build the equipment and get it to the site and get it set up. It took a lot of planning.

We needed to order a four-foot diameter by twenty-foot pipe to make the barrel of the trommel. Next, we enrolled in a welding class at the community college. We got a long piece of angle iron. We'd make a round circle with a felt marker and clamp that on the barrel. We put the torch to it and cut the hole. Then we'd turn the barrel and cut another set of holes. We probably cut a thousand two-inch holes at the large end. In the middle, that's where the small stuff fell through the one-inch holes. There were probably two thousand of those. We abandoned the two-inch holes, we found out there wasn't such a thing. It was just a story. It seemed like it took us all winter to cut them.

Then it was time to start looking for all types of new and used metal, a used welder, and six-inch water pump. We found two used water pumps and made one good one. They both had six-cylinder Chrysler engines. We used a Datson for the engine and transmission, and a three-quarter-ton International pickup for the deferential. We joined the engine and transmission to the differential of the international pickup. The wheels on the international pickup would turn when you put it in gear and turn the barrel on the trommel. The drive shafts had to be cut to proper length and welded together to turn the trommel barrel. The Datsun engine was set at ninety-degree angle to the barrel to turn the trommel.

6" Water pump

We located four sets of mobile home axels with tires so the trommel could lay in them so as they turned it would turn the trommel. Frame work was designed to support the trommel and axels. Frame work was designed to mount the engine and deferential on. The twenty-foot pipe had to have a few hundred holes cut with an acylketene torch for smaller material to fall through onto the two sluices where gold would be collected.

Trommel we designed and built.

We also built the sluice boxes. They were about 16′ long. We made three sluice boxes, but we abandoned one, we had made it for gold nuggets the size of a goose egg. It's good to be optimistic.

We rented a shed with three walls and a roof so we could work out of the weather. When it was winter in Juneau, we hung a tarp over the front and with a big construction heater we could stay reasonably warm. We purchased a flat-bed truck and a 30-foot flatbed trailer to haul most of the stuff on. We also had two utility trailers to be pulled by the pickups to haul a lot of things. We also had to purchase a Case backhoe and front-end bucket so we could move the dirt to be mined.

Winter working.

We were very excited to go to the gold fields, make our fortune, spend our winters in Hawaii, and back to mining next summer.

In the Spring we made reservations on the Alaska Marine Ferry to haul the equipment to Haines, Alaska. It would have been much shorter to go through Skagway but White Pass was not open yet because of winter snow. With the help of a couple of drivers, we got on the ferry north bound. It took seven drivers, friends of ours in Juneau, to help move all the equipment. There were two or three pickups with trailers, a truck with a trailer, a truck with a big trailer.

We also made arrangements with Canadian Customs for entering our outfit into Canada. We also took food supplies and everything we thought we'd need. Which was a huge mistake.

As we went through Haines Junction, B.C., we contacted a transport company to haul the 980 Caterpillar loader to Atlin. But we had to leave the Case backhoe in Haines, Alaska, to be moved later after we unloaded the flat-bed trailer in Atlin.

After we got the trommel off the trailer, we went back to Haines, Alaska, for the Case backhoe.

Offloading the trommel in Atlin, B.C.

Our claim was about 150-miles south of Whitehorse, which was our main supply center. However Atlin had a few food/grocery and hardware stores plus fuel.

FROM THE SAGEBRUSH OF NEW MEXICO TO THE GLACIERS OF ALASKA

When we arrived in Whitehorse, we checked in to the Yukon Inn with their big parking lot to fit all of our equipment. We contacted Customs to come inspect our stuff. We had sent them a very good itemized list but they wanted to *personally* see *everything* we had, forget the list. They had to personally see every item, one by one. This took a couple of days at top "Government Speed." When they were completely satisfied, they gave us a customs bill of $8,000.00 for Federal taxes. We realized we should have come with our shirt on our back and purchased everything there for the most part, except most of mining equipment.

It would have been cheaper to buy groceries and stuff in Canada. And then the BC Customs came to Atlin and inventoried the equipment again. Then they gave us a $4000 bill. It was US Customs in Whitehorse that gave us the $8000 bill.

After we unloaded everything off the trailer, Bobbie and I went back to Haines, Alaska, to get the Case backhoe. We had to overnight there. Leaving the next morning, we did not notice that the spare tire for the trailer was stolen. And of course, we had a flat tire about ten miles out of town. So, unhook the trailer, remove the flat tire, to take it back to Haines Junction to get it repaired. Then finally, on to Atlin gold claim.

Previously, we had purchased a construction ATCO building which had a small kitchen, bathroom, one bedroom, and a place to set up a second bed. The problem now was about 2' of snow. We spent several days plowing snow with the 980 and backhoe, clearing snow so we could move the ATCO building to its proper resting place for the summer.

ATCO trailer before it was set.

Where our camp would be, we dug a ten-foot hole by Spruce Creek. This was below the water table by the creek so it filled up part way with water. We could then pump water with a small Honda water pump and fill a three-hundred-gallon plastic tank, resting on a steel ten-foot tower. With 10′ of head pressure, we had 4-PSI of water pressure so we could use the flush toilet, run a propane water heater for washing things, and take showers. This was gentleman mining.

Later, we dug a ditch for the tires off the flatbed trailer to set in a deck alongside the ATCO trailer. We even took some old tires and stacked them, filled them with dirt, and let the sun warm the soil so we could grew a few potatoes. The weather got very warm and later on, we planted a garden for veggies. It was pretty big. This was Bobbie's job to do that. Lowell and I were preparing for mining.

ATCO "home" and garden.

Next was setting up the equipment for mining.

To refuel the equipment, we dug a trench and piled the dirt alongside it. Then we put the big fuel tank on the berm and could refuel by using gravity. A local fuel company delivered fuel as we needed it. When we went to town, we'd fill two or three barrels with gasoline for the generators and other small engines.

We had to make a big pile of dirt to set the trommel and sluice boxes on. The operation was set up on the hill that we had to build to put it on. It set at an angle so it was the right slope for the water to run out.

The setup.

First, we dug a deep hole with the backhoe and put a ladder down in it. About every 2′ we'd fill a gold pan with dirt to pan so we could see where the gold was.

If we got ten or twelve colors (specks of gold of any size), we would then strip off the over burden and mine the dirt at that level.

Lowell ran the Case and would get a load of dirt from the pit. He'd dump the dirt beside the trommel. Then he'd pick up the waste and put it elsewhere. I ran the little backhoe and would dump the gold bearing material into the trommel.

980 Caterpillar.

In the trommel was a spray-bar water pipe with a series of water nozzles running through to rinse the dirt. One inch and smaller gold nuggets would drop through the middle holes into the sluice box. We used the water pump to run the water through the trommel. Water was pumped from the creek to wash the dirt so the sluice boxes would classify and capture the gold.

Sluice boxes.

The gold bearing material would be moved over ripples to capture the gold. We called it a slick plate. It was to separate the black sand from the gold. We used a little water flow and paint brushes. There were a number of processes the girls used. They had a small sluice box and that took some of the lighter stuff and the grey sand out.

Suzanne operates the slick plate to separate the gold from the waste.

We'd clean the sluice box out every day, most minors did it about once a week. We were too anxious to find gold, so we do it every day. At end of shift, we'd have about ten gallons of 'concentrate.' We had to refine all the concentrate. That's the black sand, dirt, and gold. The gals took care of that. The next day

Bobbie and Suzanne would use other equipment to get the gold out of the concentrate.

The last thing they used was a "gold hound." It was like a dishpan that set at an angle. It had a spiral trough with water running on it so the material was picked up and carried up there. The light stuff, the sand, would wash off and the heavy stuff would drop in a hole in the back into a bucket.

In the 'gold hound,' we put the mercury to bind the gold, because it would gather all the fine gold as it tumbled around. The mercury would stick to the gold as it was heavy and it would stay in the spiral and then drop in the bucket in the back. The black sand and gold were about the same weight, we called it 'concentrate.'

Final sluice to separate the gold.

After the mercury was mixed in, we had to burn it to separate the mercury from the gold. At first we just burned it off. But we had to haul it way down the road so the wind didn't blow the mercury vapor in our face. But that was wasteful and not safe. In a sense we built a still to recover the mercury. That way we didn't have to keep buying the it.

Because the mercury would evaporate, we designed a box to catch the vapor so it would condense back to a liquid. This way we could save the mercury to get it off the gold. In order to separate them, we made a thing out of pipe. We put the concentrate in the pipe. There was a torch underneath to heat it. The vapor would travel up and go out the other end. On its way out through a pipe, we wrapped outside copper tubing and ran cold water through that so when the vapor came up it would condense back to a liquid and then drop into a glass jar at the end of the tubing. So we got the mercury back to use again. We got the mercury from mining supply places in Whitehorse.

Sometimes, the old timers would let the mercury get away. One time, when we cleaned up the sluice box, all the gold was already covered in mercury because it came in contact with some the miners had lost. We probably got more gold because it was already concentrated in the dirt we dug up.

At the end of the shift, the concentrate would be moved to the clean-up shed to further 'classify' the material until all the gold was separated from the waste material. Classify just means to separate the rocks and light weight stuff. The heavy stuff would stay in the sluice box.

Next step was weighing the gold, and wait for the gold buyer to come by and give us some money.

We had about 40 ounces, when he finally showed up. And he had a briefcase full of money. At the time it was $300 an ounce processed. The gold was actually $400 per ounce on the market, but when it comes out of the ground it's got a lot of impurities in it. So you are paid for how much pure gold there was. After they heated it and refined it, the purities would come out. There were other minerals in there as well, some of them were good, maybe platinum or whatever.

We sold the gold off as time went along rather than wait for the end of the season. When we actually stopped mining that year, I think Bobbie and I had about fifteen ounces. We just kept it because it would only net about $300 per ounce. Years later, when gold was about $800 per ounce I told Bobbie we should probably sell it. Well, it's too bad we did, because eventually it went up to $2000 or more per ounce.

This process went on all summer. Our operating expenses were about $300.00 dollars a day, so we just made expenses all summer. No Hawaii this winter. So back to the US to find a job so we could come back next summer and find a new gold field and continue our dream.

During the summer, Lee and Francelle came to visit, friends from Juneau as well as Ed and his wife Jan and their kids Trina and Brian.

The operation.

1983 (October) to 1984 (April) - Seattle and Back to Petrolane

When we got back to Seattle, I called Petrolane Gas asking for a job for the winter. This was the time in history that gasoline was so expensive. Petrolane was converting pickups and trucks to run on propane. They gave me a sales job finding companies to convert their fleet to burn propane. This was another interesting experience because sales had always been my forte. Also, I got to know the Seattle and surrounding area very good.

1984 (April) - Back to Canada and Mining the Dream

Bobbie and I purchased a 23-foot RV to live in for the summer. We traveled to Port Townsend, Washington, and took a ferry to Vancouver Island, BC. From there, we traveled up the Island to Port Hardy. Lots of beautiful country but no time to stop and enjoy it because we had to catch a ferry from Port Hardy to Prince Rupert, B.C., then the ferry to Skagway, Alaska, with a stopover in Ketchikan to visit family. The road over the Pass to B.C. was open so that saved a long trip via Haines Junction, Yukon Territory.

The previous fall Lowell and I went to Carmacks, Yukon Territory, and found a claim owner that would lease us one on shares, twenty percent of our take. This claim is one-hundred miles north of Whitehorse, then fifty miles on a dirt road to Mount Nanson, Y.T., and at 5,000' elevation.

This is so far north that the ground did not thaw until almost June. So we were very late starting by the time we got camp set up and all of our mining equipment moved, unloaded and set up. We diverted the little creek into settling a pond for our waste water to go into. In the middle of that, we made a dam to hold water back for the six-inch pump to deliver water to the trommel. In this dam, we placed our return box in the creek so the intake hose wouldn't suck all the weeds and crap into it.

The return box was an enclosed area that would fill with water and overflow into the creek but the pump wouldn't suck mud and such, because we needed clean water to flow through the trommel. To stop the water from eroding around the return box we got moss and sealed the edges to stop water from flowing past. When we peeled back the moss from the ground, there was still ice because the moss had insulated it from melting.

Now we were ready to start finding gold.

We built a covered shed for the final processing of the material. Gold buyers did not come to this forsaken place, so we had to take it to Whitehorse. It took a full day to go to Whitehorse, to sell the gold, to get supplies and fuel, and then a full day to get back to camp. So we overnighted in town. We did this every three weeks. We purchased radio-telephones so we could keep our families up to date on our adventure. These would only get a signal in certain places, so we placed a Pepsi can in that spot where we had to go to make a call. We were only 500′ from the top of Mt. Nanson, so not much snow and permafrost to provide water for the mining operation. So the season ended when the creek went dry. We had had only two months to mine.

Lowell's parents lived in Arizona and had very serious health issues, so they had to go there.

Bobbie and I had to try to dispose of all the equipment we could. Some we were able to dispose of before Lowell and Suzzanne left. We put posters up in Whitehorse and Carmacks and had a yard sale and got rid of more stuff.

The 980 loader and 10KW generator we gave to a broker in Whitehorse to sell. He sold the loader but before we got our share he declared Bankruptcy. His bank grabbed his bank account so the check he sent us bounced. I went to the Royal Canadian Mounted Police (RCMP) to press charges, because of the amount of the check I thought it would be a felony, but they tell me it is a civil matter so get an attorney. Can you imagine me getting a Canadian attorney to sue a fellow country man, me being a foreigner? I go to the bank and tried to get them to reverse that amount of money, but of course they would not. I found out the guy could legally put their home in his wife's name and his bankruptcy could not touch the house.

So, I go to broker to get relief but he was no help. He finally agreed to give me some junk equipment he had, with the argument he would pay the freight to Craig, Alaska (on Prince of Wales) and any Customs due. He gave me a 500KW Caterpillar generator and a worn-out small dozer. I had to hire a professional electrician to check them out and do some repairs. I sold the generator to a logging company. The dozer I sold for a low price to a local contractor. The broker let someone take the 10KW generator to try out, but they let it run out of oil and burned out all the crankshaft bearings. So, another loss to get resolved.

I thought I was going to get ulcers. It was a very traumatic experience. The other half of the money went to Lowell and Suzanne. They got their check before the bank grabbed his bank account. It was my fault we didn't get more money. It was my call. I should have converted the money right away, but the Canadian exchange rate was changing and I thought I'd wait another thirty days and we'd make more money. That was my mistake.

Looking back on all this, I am surprised I did not have a stroke or heart attack. However, I spent a lot of sleepless nights.

Well, by then we ran out of money, so no Hawaii again, and now we had to find a serious job to try to recoup some of our losses.

FRANK PERMENTER

1984 (November) to 2009
Prince of Wales Island – The Pioneering Years
or The Movers and The Shakers!

Once again back to Petrolane for a job. They gave me several choices, salesman in Anchorage or Seattle, I chose to go back to Southeast, Alaska, to finish the job I started several years ago to establish bulk propane deliveries on Prince of Wales Island.

That was their choice because it would be very hard for them to get someone to do that. We finally agreed on a salary. They said I would be working under the Ketchikan district. I was asking for more pay than they paid the Ketchian manager, so I suggested why not give the manager there a raise. They said they were not going to do that, and said they would send my check direct to me and not tell the manager about the pay. The manager in Ketchikan was Ed Elliott, my step-son.

Bobbie and I took our 23-foot camp trailer to POW Island to live in because nothing was available to rent or purchase.

In the daytime, we would put things from the eating table on our bed and that was my Petrolane office. At night, we put things back on the table so we had a bed to sleep on. This was in Klawock, which is seven miles from Craig and had about three times the population of Klawock. Since it was remote, people ordered everything available from the Sears catalog. Bobbie contacted Sears and got a contract to be a catalog merchant. The RV was now my Petrolane office as well as the Sears office.

I was able to convince the owner of the Black Bear convenience store in Klawock to rent me a portion of his building for my Petrolane business. Now no more shuffling things in the travel trailer. Except now Bobbie needed a store front. Guess what, I had to share my new office space with her new business.

Petrolane's business was growing at a rapid pace and so did Bobbies Sears' business. I had a desk, file cabinet, and work bench, as I worked on RV appliances. Since there were not enough places available for timber workers to rent, they lived in RVs. These RVs were made for vacations and weekend, not full time, and things soon wore out or broke. This was my job to fix or replace them, which was very good for Petrolane's business.

The pulp mill had been going for a while, but so many people came to Prince of Wales because there was so much work in the woods. There was no place for them to live, so they lived in RVs. These are designed for weekends and vacations, not full time. It was wearing them out living in them all the time. It was a great thing for us because I was selling them furnaces, working on water heaters, faucets, and door handles, all that stuff wasn't related to propane but it was a need that people had and I provided it for them. And they paid me. So I was pioneering a lot of stuff, as well as Bobbie was too.

We sold appliances and installed them as well as anything that they needed or wanted.

One time I got a call from my supervisor wanting to know why I was ordering RV toilets; they did not burn gas. I told him the customer needed it and it did not burn gas, but it paid money.

After some discussion they said go for it. Also, I learned to design and install heating systems for existing homes with gas burning appliances. Petrolane liked what I was doing because I was building a gas load for them.

It seemed everyone wanted a bulk tank for propane to get away from hauling small cylinders to be filled. Very soon I had to hire a delivery man/service man to help me. It seemed that working hours were from 'till to can't.' I loved the work and my customers loved me for providing this service.

As time went on, I thought why don't I buy this business from them? I approached the company about buying the business. Their reply was, it would not support me at this time but build the business more and they would sell it to me. Business continued to grow and finally they agreed to sell to me. I bought the inventory for $50,000. They still owned the truck and tanks.

FROM THE SAGEBRUSH OF NEW MEXICO TO THE GLACIERS OF ALASKA

Now I got a personal benefit financially. I knew I was going to need to get my own bigger place so my business had room to grow. The name for my new business became Island Propane.

We searched around and found three-acres zoned commercial for sale in Craig. I found a person to join me to purchase it. Bobbie, and I with Greg T. made an offer and then had a big scramble to get the money to complete the purchase. Between relatives and banks, Bobbie and I got money for our part as did our partner. The land was divided into lots and we and Greg selected the lots we wanted. We had to finance everything to develop it, that was to put in the street, power lines, poles and transformer, sewer lines with a lift pump because we were below the main sewer line, water lines, and lot lines. Also since it was our subdivision we named the only street. I always wanted to be on Easy street so that's what we named it- Easy Street.

Our next obstacle was to put a building on it to provide space for me and Bobbie's Sears business. The Sears business had grown so much Bobbie got a contract with Sears to become a Merchant, so now she could stock things to sell, like appliances, electronic items like TVs, etc., vacuum cleaners, and other items. We contacted a modular home builder in Centralia,

Washington, to build four modulars, 2-12' X 70' and 2-12' X 25'. Eventually they arrived by barge to Thorne Bay on the east side of the Island and, then had them delivered to Craig, on the west side, to be installed. Because of the width we had to provide pilot cars 39 miles across the Island. They were nice buildings with 6-inch walls and good insulation with double pane windows.

This all took a lot of time while both of our business continued to grow. My propane business was in one end and Sears was in the other. Now we were competing with each other for appliances. I was concerned at first but we let our customers decide where they wanted to purchase appliances. This was a good thing for the customer.

It wasn't long after we built the buildings we were able to buy a house overlooking Bucareli Bay.

After some time, we decided we needed to expand to take advantage of the way things were growing.

The Repeater Business

We got involved with a guy that was a technician for the Coast Guard. He and three or four other people in Petersburg formed a corporation. They talked Bobbie and I into buying into it. They had a repeater on top of Queen Mountain, out of Petersburg. I leased the mountain site out of Craig on Sunnahae, actually across the gully from Sunnahae. We put in our own system there. We eventually sold that to Alaska Power and Telephone.

The one in Petersburg they just disassembled it because we didn't have money to keep it going and cell phones were just coming out. It took lots of money. Our technician was a druggie, so he'd get high on drugs and one time he blow up a $500 circuit board when he was working on it. Anyway, we needed to get out of that.

Columbia helicopters flew our building and the propane tanks up there. They charged like $2500 an hour. So we loaded the tanks on one of Mitzi's trucks, one of the local freight companies in Craig. They drove out and parked it as close as they could to the base of the mountain. When the helicopter came, they just picked it up and set it down. It took only like twenty minutes, sit it was not very expensive. They built the communication shelter in the yard at Island Propane. They hauled it from there up to the top of the mountain. The shelter has the batteries in it.

The technician lived in Petersburg. If we'd have a problem in Craig, he'd have to come down and work on it. There were a lot of the problems. The batteries would go dead and they'd call me. I'd have to find a quick battery charger and get the helicopter to take me up to the top of the hill to charge the batteries. It was a mess.

The equipment was in the back of our garage. The antenna, the signal, had to come from the mountain top tot here and then it would tie into the telephone lines so you could make a phone call to New York or wherever.

FROM THE SAGEBRUSH OF NEW MEXICO TO THE GLACIERS OF ALASKA

One time I had dead batteries, and Bill, a friend from the helicopter company, came up with me to recharge the batteries. I chartered the helicopter and flew us up there. We checked the generator and I touched the plate, and it bit me. I said to Bill, "Oh that was an ouchy!"

The radio telephone we were invested in. The guy in Petersburg had three other people, and they wanted Bobbie and I to buy into it. They wanted $10,000. I told Ed S. I wouldn't loan it to them, but I'd loan it to him as a personal loan. I didn't know any of those guys, and I didn't know enough about what they were doing. When the company folded, we got most of that back. We lost money, but not as much.

Our next project was to build a new building on another lot for the propane business. When it was completed, Island Propane now had its own building. When I moved out, Bobbie contacted an office supply store in Ketchikan to get an office supply store on the Island on a commission basis. Bobbie was a long-time friend of Don and Joyce H. Between the schools and other businesses there was a big demand for office supplies. Bobbie had that business for quite a while, then the office supply store in Ketchikan decided to rent space on the Island in another location and move their business there.

Bobbie decided she wanted to sell the Sears business and sold it to one of her employees who then rented space from us. Now we named our business Island Home Center.

Then Bobbie decided she wanted to open a gift shop to sell Alaska gifts as well as all gift items, including jewelry. The vacant store space was put to use. She now has to hire two or three more people for clerks. Bobbie had always done accounting so she did all of our books.

There was a lot of real-estate activity on the Island, so Bobbie contacted a real estate office in Ketchikan to sell real estate on the Island thru their office. She took classes to get her agent license. She could not hang a sign and open her office without a broker present, so after two years she was able to get her broker's license. Then she opened her own office "POW Island Realty." All of our businesses continued to grow and both Bobbie and I had to hire more help. I now had three besides myself and Bobbie had five or six.

We were both very busy but we made time to get involved in community activities. We got involved with a few others to establish the first Chamber of Commerce. And both of us were Chamber presidents at one time or another.

There are a lot of islands around Ketchikan and some had Forest Service cabins to use. Now the cabins are not there anymore, the USFS made them go away. In the old days we would rent one of them and go there for a few days to fish. Sometimes we'd take a couple of friends and spend a lot of time fishing. Mostly for cutthroat trout or rainbow trout. And lots of R and R. (resting and relaxing).

Fishing with Donnie and his wife Betty in Juneau.

Every year there was a salmon derby and I always bought a ticket but never caught a big enough fish to enter. The one year I did not buy a ticket and guess what, I caught a forty-eight-pound salmon...so it goes. That was sure a disappointment. I would have won the derby that day The pot was $10,000. A lot of people bought tickets for it.

We took a lot of boat trips with others in their boat, and many times it was for the weekend. Summer times was wonderful for fishing and crabbing.

FROM THE SAGEBRUSH OF NEW MEXICO TO THE GLACIERS OF ALASKA

I joined the Coast Guard Auxiliary and learned a lot of boating skills. The Coast Guard Auxiliary is a group of enthusiasts that want to learn boating safety. The Coast Guard promotes it a lot because it makes their job easier. They had an election, I wanted to join the Auxiliary but I didn't want to be the president. I did allow myself to be elected vice president because there wasn't very many people in it. A month or two later, the president who was a school teacher, was transferred somewhere else, so I became the Commander. We would hold safety classes for boating and inspect boats. We inspected a lot of boats. That was lot of fun and where I gained a lot of my boating knowledge.

One day while on vacation, I went to the plant to get our vehicle fuel. I heard someone yelling and saw a skiff floating down the channel. Realizing someone was in trouble I told my wife Bobbie to call the Coast Guard and ran down to our dock where there was a small skiff moored. I jumped in just as my service man arrived and we went to where we could see a man's head out of the water. When we arrived, we were able to get him in the skiff.

He told us he had a small outboard with the gas tank on the motor. So But while trolling, he was trying to refuel the tank when a small wake came by causing gasoline to spill on the motor. This caused a fire and some gasoline spilled on his pants leg and caught on fire, so he panicked and jumped overboard with no life jacket on. Well, the skiff drifted away and he had on boots and heavy clothing so he couldn't swim to the skiff. When we picked him up, he said he was so tired he was about to give up and sink.

When we arrived at the dock the Coast Guard had arrived with a diver dressed to go in the water with dive gear on. This was a lucky day for this gentleman and we felt wonderful that we were there to save him.

One time I worked for the Census Bureau on Prince of Wales. This was the 2000 census. We had to go to every house as everyone was supposed to be contacted. But some of them weren't home, some of them wouldn't give me any information. When it was over, in 2001, we had to go back and do cleanup of those that we didn't get information from. They flew us to Anchorage to train us for the cleanup. I had two or three people working with me.

There was a family was living in a float house south of Hydaburg and I had to charter a plane to go down there and contact them. Smith Cove was another place where some people lived. They weren't there so I had to go back to see them. Another one was in Edna Bay. I went there, they were real reluctant to give me any information, but they finally did. Then there was a guy in Thorne Bay that I never could get any information from. He just flat refused to do it, "I'm not giving the government nothing." I explained why the Census Bureau needed it but he didn't care. For the most part I got most of them cleaned up. We had a friend who had a float plane and the Census Bureau would charter him to fly us.

One time FBI's Ten Most Wanted team showed up in Thorne Bay. If I was in that kind of condition I wouldn't go to a place like Thorne Bay, I'd go to New York or LA where there's lots of people to hide in plain sight. When the bad guy came to Thorne Bay, my goodness they hadn't hardly put foot on land before someone recognized that they were outlaws and called the FBI. They arrested them right away. Any kind of stranger shows up, you recognize them as not a local.

Bobbie eventually sold the gift shop to one of her employees. They rented space for it from us.

We were recouping our losses from mining, so we learned it was better to mine people than mine for gold.

We both had super employees and were finally able to take some time off. It was slow in February, so we started going to Maui for the month. We did this for several years.

March is a wet month. It's when winter is trying to turn loose and spring is trying to come in. February was a bad month business-wise, but March is when it was nasty weather. We'd spend most of February on Maui, and then we'd come back in March and think, "What are we doing here!"

Also, we did lots of fishing on the weekends. Some of the best fishing in the world for salmon and halibut, that is my opinion. The salmon going to spawn and swim right past POW Island. Also, lots of bottom fish.

Deer hunting was very good and we had fish and venison in our freezer all the time. We were allowed four deer a piece each year.

After I had sold the propane business I thought I retired. But instead, we built another building and I opened an appliance store. Well, we befriended a fellow and he became a good friend. We let him sleep in a sleeping bag in the store so he didn't have to rent a place. When we went out of town, he'd stayed there in case somebody wanted to buy something. That way he could sell it to them. But anytime anyone wanted to go fishing, I was available.

Arrowhead Transfer was a local freight company that had operations in Sitka, Petersburg, and Craig. One day, Gordy H., the owner of Arrowhead, stopped by and asked if I was interested in selling my propane business. He needed more for the employees to do because the freight business was not enough to keep his employees busy, and they could do both businesses. I said I had not thought about it but would talk to Bobbie and let him know. We were approaching retirement age and decided to sell. We notified Gordy of this and he wanted to know how much. We told him and he thought it was a reasonable price, and did we want cash or terms. I needed to consult our accountant to tell him because at the time President Clinton was considering raising Capital Gains. Our accountant told us if it did change it would be retroactive and we would be stuck for higher taxes. So, we asked for cash. "Bird in the hand is better than two in the bush" so to speak.

Eventually we rented the propane building to a greenhouse nursery business and I was out of a job. Bobbie did not want to retire so we built another building and I opened an appliance and electronic store in one half of the new store. It was still Island Home Center. I was now on social security and my net profits did not affect my social security check. Then we rented the other half to a person that was looking for space to open a pharmacy. This space was a perfect fit for he and his wife, both of them were pharmacists.

Walmart had moved into Ketchikan and changed the Island. People on Prince of Wales could go over and back on the ferry in one day. So people going in to Ketchikan would shop at Walmart and that cut into my sales. and some of the businesses on Prince of Wales went out of business. When I sold appliances, this one guy from Hollis came in looking for a dryer. He said, "I'm gonna go into town and check their prices." But he came back and bought from me. He said, "Your prices are cheaper than theirs in there." I kept my prices down for that very reason. Otherwise, I wouldn't have ever sold anything. Better to have one in your hand than two in the bush. Amazon and Costco are doing that to our country too. Later I sold my business to an appliance repair company in Klawock.

I finally convinced Bobbie it was time to retire, or actually, she was envious of me fishing in the 25-foot cabin cruiser we had purchased, and she was working, she loved to fish also.

After I retired, one of the charter guys who had a 25' cabin cruiser and had a bad wrist said he couldn't fish anymore. He said, "If my boat doesn't work one day it cost me $1500." He had a spare part for everything that could go wrong on the boat, of course I bought all those. If something needed to be done in one hundred hours, he'd do it in fifty hours. Everything was in top shape. It had a bulkhead, a door to walk in the cabin, a canvas over the back part.

We did a lot of fishing and hunting when time permitted. Some of the best fishing in the world, I think, is the waters off Prince of Wales Island. The salmon swam right past our island and it was lots of fun all summer when someone would go with me. I never went fishing alone but lots of friends and family came to visit. I always made time to take them out so they took lots of fish home. We always kept fish and venison in our freezer. We would see lots of humpback whales and orcas on every trip, also sea lions on some of the points that looked like Newport, Oregon.

Addington Point was always covered with sea lions. It was always an interesting point besides the sea lions, it's also where the riptides were. When the tides would change, they are not like a wave, they're up and down. All you could do was just idle through them. Pretty soon you would get through. Then you can take off again. It scared me. It scared the heck out of me the first time I did it. This was in the twenty-five foot then.

FROM THE SAGEBRUSH OF NEW MEXICO TO THE GLACIERS OF ALASKA

Those sea lions loved to strip the salmon off our line. One time I had a big salmon on and I had him worn down and almost to the boat when my reel started emptying. So I knew it was a sea lion. I set the dray real heavy and pretty soon my line went slack and I reeled in a perfect set of salmon gills. I should have had mounted them on a board for conversations later. I wish I had a lot of times. It would have been unusual to see a plaque with a perfect set of gills.

When we were in Craig, the herring would swim by and spawn, and they lay their eggs on the kelp. It only happens in February. The kelp grows everywhere out in the salt water and usually it's not in deep water, just around close to the islands. Everybody knows what kelp is. Another one comes along and lays his eggs on it. It'll get built up three, four, or five layers thick. Then they'll take the kelp leaves off. You can eat them. I like them with soy sauce. You eat the whole thing, leaf and all.

Sometime commercially, they put out hemlock branches. I don't care for the taste of the hemlock needles. They'll take Styrofoam logs or anything that floats, and make a big square. They put an anchor on it so it stays in place. Then they hang lines down from it. They'll go harvest kelp and tie it to the lines. The herring come by and then spawn on the kelp. They get $10 or $20 a pound. The Japanese especially like to eat it. It's good.

Sometimes I would motor along in the boat, reached down into the ocean, pull out a kelp leaf, looks at it, then maybe take a chomp out of it. If it didn't have enough roe on it, I'd throw it back and putter along to the next leaf. Sometimes the leaf already has a couple of bites taken out of it. I'd bite and throw them back until I found a leaf I liked.

When we became snowbirds, I tried to get people to harvest it for me and I'd buy it from them. But they wouldn't do it. Bobbie would melt butter and put soy sauce in a pan, and we would just dunk the leaf in it. I even like a little green tabasco sauce, but mostly soy sauce.

(I like fried pork skins. I get a bag of them once in a while. Anne only kind of likes them, I'm glad she doesn't like them very well.)

Another time I took friends Pat and Dez M., halibut fishing. Dez was in a wheelchair, but got around okay. Pat caught a huge halibut. She wrestled for a long time and finally got it to the surface. I got my harpoon ready and told her to loosen the drag but keep her thumb on the reel because when I stuck that harpoon in him, he was going to be very angry and want to go back home deep down. I had a 16-inch buoy on the end of the harpoon line and the halibut took that buoy down and it stayed for a long time. I thought the buoy had burst but after a while it popped up and Pat still had him on her line. so I trolled toward him and she reeled till he got back to the boat, then I told her the same thing to hold her thumb on the reel because I was going to shoot him with my little pistol.

When I shot him, the water turned red with blood but he tried to go back to the bottom. I was concerned the sea lions would flock in but they didn't. Now he is too big for us to lift into the boat. I tied him off on a boat cleat and trolled slowly to another fisherman nearby and he helped us get him in the boat. When we got to the dock, we found he was too long to reach the scales and get off the dock to weight him. Instead, we measured him to determine his weight, which came out to 268 pounds. WHEW!!!!

Bobbie finally sold her real estate business, and then we purchased a Ram diesel and a 30-foot 5th wheel and became snow birds.

There were two school teachers that lived on a sail boat we got to live in our house we had purchased in Craig. They had a new baby and a sail boat is not a good place to live in the wet, windy, and cold winter. We let them live in our house in the winter to keep anything from freezing for just the utilities. It was prefect for them and wonderful for us. Eventually we sold them our house, which was on a hill just above Bucarelli Bay, almost an inside ocean, 25 miles from the Gulf of Alaska with some islands in between it and us.

Now we had the best of both worlds, Alaska in the summer and Arizona in the winter.

When we lived in Yuma, we'd go to Laughlin at least once a winter and overnight. Pretty soon we were getting free nights because we were gambling.

FROM THE SAGEBRUSH OF NEW MEXICO TO THE GLACIERS OF ALASKA

Bobbie had a brother who lived in Bullhead City across the river. There was a ferry that would run back and forth from Bullhead City to Laughlin. Then the gambling places had cheap meals, $3.99. Her brother would just take the ferry over, have dinner, and come back home. It's not like that now, you pay well for your dinner. They got greedy!

Sometimes we'd go to Yuma in November, and it was pretty good it was still warm. Not hot but warm. In December and January, even February, it was actually cold sometimes. If you didn't leave by May it was triple digits.

This would have been somewhere in the early 2000s. Deadhorse is five miles from Prudhoe Bay but you had to go on a tour for security reasons. You could sit there and look at Prudhoe Bay but we didn't actually physically go there. We drove the Haul Road, Dalton Highway. You go out of Fairbanks, part of way up you go to Coldfoot which is a truck stop or convenience store, gas and diesel station. It's about the only business on that whole highway. Then you get to the Brooks Range and go over the mountains. They are some pretty rugged mountains. Then you go from there, it's nearly all the way across the country, down to the Arctic plains. You even see muskox.

The thing that impressed me a lot, it's just flat ground, there's no tall brushes or anything, just short shrubs. They get a lot of snow sometimes, so there are these tall poles on the side of the road. And here's a hawk, hanging off the side of the pole looking around for something to catch. We camped in the Brooks Range. We even went to Inuvik in the Northwest Territories. Going from Dawson City, that's where the gold rush was, just before that there's a fork in the road that goes to Inuvik, five-hundred seventy-five miles or so on just a gravel road. Bobbie and I had our pull trailer then.

When I first was transferred to Juneau, I joined the Lions Club. They held a convention there one year and there were some people from Inuvik. They were the most fun people. I thought, 'I gotta go to Inuvik.' It's in the oil fields, there's lots of gas and oil wells. It's right on the Beaufort Sea, so they do some fishing. Most jobs are related to the oil and gas fields and fishing. The Mackenzie River dumps into the Beaufort Sea. It's a muddy river, so it makes the whole sea muddy. The whales are beluga and they're white. We chartered a small plane to do a sightseeing tour. You could see the pods of beluga, the oil rigs and gas rigs, and a lot of small islands.

We went with Dorothy and Shep to Fairbanks. There we took a bus tour to go across the Arctic Circle. Then we went on to Dawson City. It's right on the Yukon River. You cross the Yukon from Dawson City and go Top Of The World highway. This is in Yukon Territory. This is where the fork in the road goes to Inuvik. We didn't see much wildlife. In the Brooks Range we saw caribou. We just wanted to go there and see what it was. We went to Prudhoe Bay from Fairbanks. The Haul Road is around three-hundred miles, most of it gravel.

We took the ferry one time from Ketchikan to Hyder. We've also come in from the Canadian side. Both Bobbie and I, and Anne and I. When we were there the salmon weren't running. But there's viewpoint, a platform over the river and you can watch the fish and bear. Twice there wasn't a salmon run. Anne and I drove up the road out of Hyder, way up to the very top as far as you could go. It's all gravel and kind of rough. There's a beautiful glacier up there, the Salmon Glacier near Stewart , B.C. It comes down out of the mountains and then it forks. One part goes to Canada and the other part comes on down to the water. There was an old guy that would come up there from New Jersey or somewhere, he was a bear guide and he'd tell you all about the bear. That was one of the most beautiful place I've ever seen.

We took many RV trips in the summer with friends from Alaska. We went to about every place in Alaska and Canada we could drive to Denali Park, Prudhoe Bay, Dawson City, Inuvik, Yukon Territory, Yellowknife, Y. T., and of course Fairbanks, Anchorage, and Kenia Peninsula. Also Wrangell-St. Elias National Park. In the winter we went to Grand Canyon, Tucson, Corpus Cristy, San Antonia, Padre Islands, Mexico, and lots of places in-between. We purchased a lot in Yuma and put a modular on it for our home when not traveling or in Alaska. We also added a metal covered shed for the 5th wheel that we used for a guest house when not traveling, because we had lots of company from Alaska. We absolutely loved our new life.

FROM THE SAGEBRUSH OF NEW MEXICO TO THE GLACIERS OF ALASKA

We joined an RV caravan of 15 vehicles on an 18-day trip down the Baja. Since it only about eight-hundred miles, there was lots of time to sight see along the way. One side trip was by panga, I call a skiff, to a bay off the Pacific where whales came to give birth to their babies. The Moms were so proud of their young they brought them alongside of the panga and we were able to put our hand on mom or baby. This was the coolest thing I had ever experienced. The whales were cold and slimy to touch.

One place where they processed abalone, the beautiful shells were stockpiled about 8' high and a mile or two long out on this peninsula. The roads in the RV park were paved with them. Of course, we took a bucket full home with us.

2006 – Australia

When we were on our Australia New Zealand trip. Auckland there was one of the hotels that they had built a patio on about the fifteenth floor. You're up there looking all over or you can look straight down.

Australia and New Zealand was 2006. This guy we knew from Ketchikan liked to travel and he put these trips together. He'd get a free trip by having so many people in a group. He would pick out several places and make arrangements. This one trip was to be from Ensenada to Tahiti, from Tahiti to all the Hawaiian Islands, and then fly back. About a week or two before the trip, they broke the ship and canceled the cruise.

They gave us a choice of four places that we could take in place of that cruise. Of course we took Australia and New Zealand because those are super spendy if you have to go buy them. He made reservations for us on the phone in Sydney. We were screwed up pretty much when we get to Sydney because we had to cross six time-zones and the International dateline.

But when we got to Sydney, we found out we didn't have any reservations. We had left before they confirmed one way or the other. They finally did find us a place to stay and we had a couple of days before our trip. But we were just numb, really numb.

We toured around Sydney for a couple of days. I wanted to go to the reef off of Australia but it's quite a ways north from Sydney. We got back on the boat and went to Melbourne. It took a day or two to get there. We got to spend a whole day in Melbourne, but it's like Sydney, it may be bigger or smaller but they're both huge. It would take you all day just to get out of town, let alone do anything and get back on the boat. So we just stayed in town.

We were so amazed at the transportation system over there. There were busses, trolley cars, rail cars, and street cars, so you could get around without a vehicle. Probably because there's so many people there. We just got to see shops in town.

From there we traveled across to Tasmania, which is an island on the other side of Australia. We didn't get off the boat, we just went there to fuel up.

Then we headed across the Tasmanian Sea, going to New Zealand, it was two or three full days

crossing that sea. It was a long way. We stopped at Christchurch. That's the supply point for Antarctica. After we were there, and before Kathy went there with her singing group, they had a real bad earthquake that wiped out the town. We got to spend a day or two. One of the things we did, we went on this one tour, they dressed you up in parkas, boots, and gloves, and they put you in an argo, which is a six-wheeled all-terrain vehicle for Antarctica. They pull a couple of those behind a tug. It can crossover the ice. We got to see what it was like to be in Antarctica but we didn't have to go there.

We stopped at one or two other towns in New Zealand. We got to Auckland, which I think is the capital of New Zealand, but it's on the far end of the island. There they parked the cruise ship on a pier. There's a channel, and the America's Cup sailboats were going past, as far as from me to across the street, from us. But the race was going to be five-miles offshore. For quite a few bucks you could go on the boat and watch it. We had two or three days to wait for our train, so we had a hotel. Anne and I were on the nineteenth floor. We were looking out the window and there's the sailboat out there. It was quite a ways out, but with a binoculars you could see it pretty good. We called everybody that was in our group, there was about a dozen of us. They all came down and brought libations, and we sat there and watched the race out the motel window.

There wasn't much to do there. I went down and gathered some rocks from New Zealand and took home with me.

The cruise was in February. In March I had my knee done.

I got to see a lot of the world. I would have liked to have gone to Switzerland or someplace like that. Iceland seemed to be a pretty popular destination.

2010 - 2015
Canby – An End of an Era

After we moved to Canby, we were renting out 5000-square foot of building space and got a dollar a square foot in rent. In the ten years we had them, we received as much as it was worth. But we eventually sold in 2010 or 2011.

Eventually our life style crashed. Bobbie had colon cancer while still in Alaska, but became cancer free for several years. But by 2010, her health had detreated to the point we had to sell out of Yuma as well as Alaska, We moved to Canby where all of Bobbie's children lived nearby in the area and bought a house. The colon cancer was coming back along with some heart problems. This was a drastic change from our past life style. But we were very blessed to have a loving family and friends for support. God had blessed us all of our life and still does.

Very sad on all accounts.

Ed and I went back to Yuma and spent a month or so selling our place and hauling back as much of our personal possessions as would fit in my pickup. While doing that, we did a lot of golfing and tourist stuff in southern Arizona. Bobbie and I had previously sold the last of our property in Alaska. We rented a house in Canby for a year until we purchased the one we now live in.

With our traveling was over, I looked after Bobbie, joined a golf club, and worked in my wood shop to keep busy. Bobbie passed away in 2014. We had gotten a little Boston Terrier we named George and he continued to be my shadow. He and I became more attached now. George and I took several trips in our RV but not much fun, so I stopped that for a while.

The family and I took her ashes to Ketchikan to scatter in the Revilla Channel in front of the house where she had spent many years and raised her family.

There are so many places that Bobbie and I went to, and Anne and I have gone to different ones. I think we drove every road in Alaska, up to Yellowknife in the Yukon Territory, everything from there we went on every road you could drive on and every road you could drive on in Alaska. The Canadian Rockies is really a beautiful place. There's still a lot of stuff out there I'd like to see.

By the time I reached here, I was pretty much tired of writing my story.

I just wanted it to be done.

Or so I thought.

2015 - 2024
Canby – The Beginning of New Adventures

I had a neighbor that was a hand therapist. Janet, and we became friends. She had a patient from Salem (thirty miles from Canby) that was getting therapy from her at Woodburn. The patient was Anne Beckett.

Anne was complaining to Janet that she could find only culls for a mate, so Janet told her she sounded like her neighbor. Janet asked Anne if she would like to give me her phone number. Anne thought what the heck why not, except he had to be a Christian and a Republican. Janet told her she thought I was both, and gave me Annes phone number. I gave her a call later. We talked for about forty-five minutes and made a lunch date for Sunday. This had to be a Divine Intervention because I never went to Salem and Anne never came to Canby. We would not have ever met. We were blessed again.

We met for lunch and visited the rest of the afternoon. It seemed that we were almost 100% same in our likes and dislikes. This was September 6th, 2015, and we got married on December 6th, 2015. We were in, "hog heaven," as the saying goes.

Frank and Anne.

We spent our honeymoon in the house that Anne and her past husband Dick had purchased that was on a lot on the beach in Pacific City, Oregon, where they had built a three-bedroom, two-bath home. The ocean was only a few feet away. Now we are in paradise so to speak.

FROM THE SAGEBRUSH OF NEW MEXICO TO THE GLACIERS OF ALASKA

Frank on the beach at Pacific City.

Anne has two children; Andy Pitt and Loren Gearhart. Both live in or near Wilsonville within 15 or 20 miles from us in Canby. Andy is a Dermatologist and Lauren a doctor specializing in Internal Medicine. It seems Andy is forever cutting basal-cell cancers from my head. Anne has had two-years nurses training so I am well looked after medically. Both Anne and I took CPR training so we could use it if ever necessary.

Anne sold her Salem house and bought into mine in Canby. Ever try to incorporate furnishings from two three-bedroom houses into one? Cannot be done. So we gave away a lot of stuff. We both hated yard sales, so better to give away and be done with it.

Anne and I made frequent trips to the beach house over the next several years. Our first trip out of state was to Safari Convention in Las Vegas with Andy, (he is a big game trophy hunter). All the animals from around the world were stuffed and displayed there. This was the most interesting thing I had ever seen. Also, we saw a couple of interesting shows. One was a magician and the other was Carrot Top.

We both liked to travel so we did a lot of that, mostly in our RV.

Frank and Anne cruising.

Next we took a RV trip through the Redwoods in California, then on to central California to visit some of our relatives in Fresno and Bakersfield. Then on to Palm Springs and Yuma for a week or two in the warmth. We even took short day trips into Mexico as tourists. On the way back home, we went to Lake Powell and Antelope Canyon. Wonderful and indescribable to see. On same trip we went to Bryce Canyon and Zion Park. Next would be the Air Show in Reno.

Debbie and her husband, Bert, house was close enough we had a big barbecue and watched the air show.

One time Anne and I tried to go to Oatman, Arizona coming in from the west side. The highway sign said if you're more than 30′ long don't go. So we went around and came in from the south. We just drove through town, there were so many people there. They were feeding the Burros. We just drove through town and turned around and came back. We didn't even park.

2016 - Queen Charlotte Islands for Fishing

June 30th we took a quick trip to California to Leon and Dodie's 60th anniversary. Then in August we had contractor build large extension over deck in back.

Frank at home in the back yard.

I went fishing with Andy, and his friend Gary, north of Queen Charlotte Island, now called Haida Gwaii, British Columbia, for a week. The weather was not good but we caught a few fish.

Gary was a handyman on Andy's wheat ranch in central Oregon doing odds and ends around his place. We flew to Vancouver, then caught a plane from there that was owned by the lodge. We flew to a bush airport with not a lot of amenities. The plane was like a 737, it was a nice plane. There were about six helicopters that we flew on. The flight was only about twenty minutes to the lodge. The fish processing was offshore with a floating boardwalk out to it. It used to be a whaling place where they processed whales, boiling them down after they caught them. After we landed the helicopter, we were greeted by the people to make you feel really good. They were really nice to us. You go in the lodge and there's a hospitality room. This table's got wine, that one's got hard liquor, everybody socializes for an hour. Then go in the dining room and it was good food. We kind of lie to each other, you know how that goes.

There's people from all over the USA and Canada on this trip. There were seventeen of us. The next morning we go out, but it's kind of nasty weather. We caught a few fish, but not very many. The next day it was really nasty. We went out but it was not comfortable at all. The third day we didn't even go. We spent all that money, no fish but it was fun.

The Queen Charlotte Islands at Langara. The next one we went to in Canada was on Graham Island off the Queen Charlotte's. The first one we went to was Graham Island. This was with Andy and Gary.

Two or three years later we went back in the same area, Langera, it's an island off what used to be called the Queen Charlotte's. They changed it to an Indian name. The lodge was kind of nice. We caught halibut and salmon. The orcas were in, so we had them playing around us. We caught one halibut that must have been close to three-hundred pounds. We didn't put it in the boat. I tried to take pictures but it was underwater so he didn't show up. We did catch some smaller halibut. We caught some salmon. I caught a thirty-one-pound salmon, it was the biggest one.

That night at the dinner table, I got a little ribbon as champion.

We flew in from the same airport in the helicopter. There was a float in front of this real steep mountain about 300′ high. It had the fish processing, cleaning, boxing, and vacuum sealing. There was a tram that went all the way up the mountain. That's how we got up to where the lodge was. Then you can walk around on a deck and look down, it was pretty neat.

In September Ryan, Bobbies grandson, and his high school buddies invited me to go deer hunting at Maupin for a week. That was beginning of an annual event, and to me that was very special. We got mule deer in Maupin. Then we started getting elk tags. One year we got four elk tags for bulls and got those.

The next year we got three elk tags. But I didn't use my tag because by then I was getting old.

In October Anne and I purchased a new Arctic Fox travel trailer and sold our old one. November 12th to California to my Aunt Nells 100th birthday. December was a quiet month at home to end 2016.

2017 – Okay, No Big Adventures

January 2017 was mostly therapy for my shoulder rotator cuff repair. February Anne and I left with RV to Arizona for a month or two. We visited and was a tourist in 29 Palms and Palm Springs. Then on to Yuma for a while. Followed by Phoenix then Death Valley and points of interest in between.

One the way back, we stopped in Reno where my daughters live, Debbie, Bobbie, and Pat, for a few days. Then back to home in Canby.

Annes birthday was on the 10th of April. May spent at home and some time at beach house in Pacific City. June 21st to 28thwe took the RV to the Permenter Reunion in California. July was at home in Canby and Beach house.

Most every Tuesday I mowed pastures at Andy's place on Ladd Hill Road. He has twenty acres and about half of it in grass. I used a Kubota with a flail mower about once a month in summer.

August 11th to Grants Pass for my oldest brothers 90th birthday. Then September 18th to Idaho to visit friends in Hayden and Sandpoint.

October and November were quiet months.

Dec 6th was Anne and our 2nd wedding anniversary, and a wonderful two years with the love of my life.

2018 - All Over The Country

January 25, 2018, we left for Bakersfield to Aunt Aggies memorial service. Then on to Yuma for the annual Howling At Moon Party. There are probably a thousand-plus people out in the desert. They set up a flat-bed trailer for a stage for the musicians. They'd rake rocks from an area of about 100' square on the ground for a dance floor. It was jammed with couples dancing. Everyone brought their own food and libations. It was a huge unbelievable party and everyone had a ball. No lights, everyone brought their own chairs, porta potties were provided. The new moon came up over the mountain and everyone howled at the moon. This has become an annual January tradition in Yuma, mostly snow birds but many locals have joined in.

From there to Mesquite, Nevada to visit friends, then home with a couple of days stopover in Reno with my daughters.

June 6th we left with friends in four RVs for a couple of months in Canada and Alaska. Took in all the sights along the way. We did some halibut fishing in Homer, Alaska. We chartered a small plane in Talkeetna for an hour to fly over and around all the glaciers and mountains in and around Mount McKinley, now called Denali. There was not a cloud anywhere. A very breath-taking trip, once in a life time experience. We saw lots of wild animals, goats, sheep and moose.

In Skagway, we rode the narrow-gauge railroad up White Pass, the path of the 1998 gold rush trail to Dawson, Yukon Territory.

Frank in the small airplane flying to Mt. McKinley.

On the same trip we visited Atlin B.C., where I had mined in 1983. The area had been clear cut of timber and mined so nothing was familiar.

FROM THE SAGEBRUSH OF NEW MEXICO TO THE GLACIERS OF ALASKA

In September Anne and I went with Canby Adult Center to Washington, DC, and took in all of tourist sites in the area. We saw Arlington Cemetery and the Washington Monument. What I liked about it was, we flew back on a plane, then a bus took us everywhere so we didn't have to park. We walked a lot but it was very interesting.

December 1st it was elk hunting in central Oregon and we brought home four elk.

2019 – Fishing Amazon River Basin in Brazil

January 19th we left Canby in our RV for Yuma. I had a dentist appointment in Algodones, Mexico. Mexico has some very good dentists. We and many of our friends and relatives have been using Mexico dentists and the price is about one-third the price at home. They are well trained and do very good work. Also, a very interesting place to visit. The people are very poor in Mexico, but love the money the snow birds bring.

On the way back to Canby we went to Fairfield, California to visit a good friend from Ketchikan who is in a care home there.

Brazil

In November Andy and I went to Brazil to fish the Amazon Basin. We caught lots of Peacock Bass and other species.

We caught piranhas. The camp we stayed in was on an island in the river. It was a jungle, and the island didn't have as much vegetation on it. We fished out of skiffs. We'd go fish until noon, then everyone would take naps, and then we'd go fish again. We were there a week or ten days. We caught lots of fish. There were a dozen cabins on stilts for when the river flooded. It rained so much it can get 10' deep where there wasn't any water before. They had an area called the Liars Table. It was built out over the river. The table was made out of a tree that they sawed and each chair was made from a tree stump. It was called the Liars Table because we had a waitress that served us drinks and everyone told stories. There was a place where they brought us dinner and we ate the local cuisine, but there was nothing special about the meals. A TV dish was mounted so that we could get it if we wanted to. I never did. There were about a dozen people there with us. Although it was November, we were below the equator just south of Venezuela, it wasn't cold. This was in the Amazon River Basin.

We flew into Manaus, the capital and largest city in the Brazilian state of Amazonas. There we walked the streets sightseeing. It was a very, very poor country, electric wires scrambled around, broken up sidewalks. Then we went to a shopping center that was top scale. There's rich people and poor people in Brazil. And we got to see a little bit of both.

There we took a bus that took us to the waterfront. Where we were rowed across the Rio Negro River which is black from the needles and leaves to the Amazon river. The Rio Negro was black and the Amazon was gray. It took about a mile or two for all the colors to blend together. When we landed, we rode a bus for an hour or more, then we got in a skiff and rode upstream for about an hour to the lodge where we stayed.

One night they took us for a jungle tour. We went out with a flashlight to see a crocodile-like animal but it was only about 3' long. They would go over on the beach and capture them. Then they would bring them back on the skiff and we could hold them. There was no light, just the flashlight to shine in their eyes. Another night they had canoe rides, but neither Andy nor I did that.

Andy usually would arrange side trips, something to do besides fishing.

2020 - COVID Didn't Stop Us!

The 19th of February we flew back to Cape Coral to visit one of Annes best friends for a week or so. While there we took about 4 days to visit Key West, Florida. Then flew back to Canby. We went to Cape Coral twice.

The east coast of Florida is amazing. The temperature of the water is warm because the currents go up the East Coast. When we went near Orlando where Ty was stationed with the Coast Guard, we went to the beach. The water was actually a little bit warm. That was our second trip to Cape Coral. We flew on Southwest, because we had free passes because Debbie worked there. We went to Fort Myer and Anne's long-time friends picked us up at the airport.

FROM THE SAGEBRUSH OF NEW MEXICO TO THE GLACIERS OF ALASKA

The next time we drove in. The first time we went back there we didn't do that much sightseeing. The next time we went, we had the pickup because we left our trailer in Mission, Texas. That was an interesting trip because we spent three or four days going to Key West.

The other time, we'd gone to Yuma with the fifth wheel and met up with a friend that had been one of my propane dealers from Wrangle. We went with them to Nogales to an art show. Then we left them and went to Carlsbad Cavern in New Mexico. Then to Mission, Texas, where Anne's good friend from Canby spent their winters. Then we went on to Florida. From there we went to Key West and spent a couple of three days sight-seeing there. Once we got back to Cape Coral, we went to wear Ty (Bobbie's grandson) was in the Coast Guard and spent a few days touring the east coast of Florida.

On the way back to Texas, we stopped at Avery Island in Louisiana where Tabasco is made. Avery Island is in Louisiana on I-10. They make so much stuff and they ship it all over the world. I didn't realize there were so many different kinds of Tabasco. Most of it you don't see in the stores around here. We spent a day or two there. Then back to Mission where we had dropped our trailer. We toured through New Mexico and went to the old homestead, but it was fenced off and we couldn't walk up to it. We were gone a couple of months.

March we were at home all month. We each got COVID and we were pretty much homebound. We hardly would go out, we just stayed home.

In April we drove to Las Vegas, Nevada, for my friend Boone Myers Memorial.

July, we took a RV trip to Eastern Oregon to visit many nature sites.

In August Anne had heart valve replaced. She had a stroke after the surgery and spent a couple of weeks in the hospital for therapy and recovery. The day I was supposed to bring her home, wild fires came close enough to cause us to pack up and be ready to evacuate. Fortunately we did not have to.

December, I had my second knee replaced so therapy and discomfort for the next year but now good knee.

2021 - Fishing the Bayous

January was a very quiet month.

Mississippi and Louisianna

But in July Andy and I flew to Biloxi, Mississippi, to fish the bayous and in the Gulf of Mexico.

We caught a lot of catfish in Louisiana. It was July and hot!

We stayed on a barge that was the headquarters for the company we were fishing with. We fished the bayou's and Mississippi River. From there we went to Biloxi, Mississippi, and fished in the Gulf of Mexico. We fished for a week. We caught Red Snapper, and a fish they just called Red Fish but they were eatable and quite a few of them. We brought lots of fish home. We brought home three coolers full of fish. We're still eating them. We stayed in a hotel a block from Bourbon Street. That was $500 or something a night. We had a great time.

September back to Yuma, with a side trip through the redwoods in Oregon and California.

Then we took a week trip to Reno to visit the daughters and my birthday party. October 27th I turned 90 and feeling good and look forward to 100.

Frank 80th Birthday.

2022 - Fishing Around the World

Andy, Crystal (Anne's granddaughter), Anne and I went to Brownlee Reservoir in eastern Oregon. We went fishing but we didn't get any. Well, we did get one fish, but when we were transferring it from the boat to the dock, it fell in. While in Eastern Oregon we went to Painted Hills and Pendleton. Debbie came along with us.

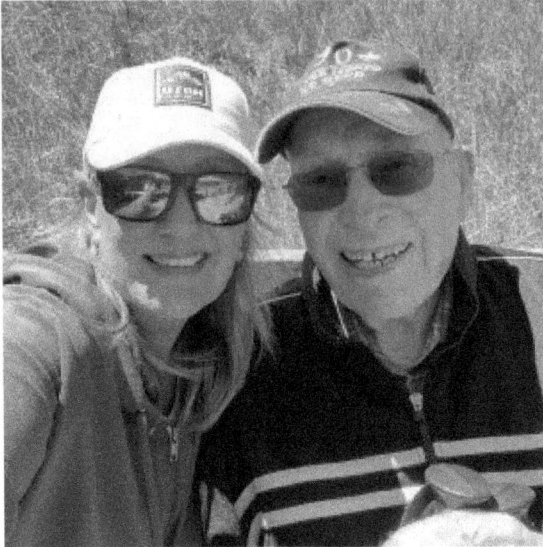

Debbie and Frank.

Fishing on Odell Lake, which is up Willamette Pass, did work out as planned. Andy had rented a house up there, it was about $700 a day or something like that. Pretty nice house. It was Andy, Crystal, Anne, and I. We went fishing with a guy the first day. He showed us where they were. The next day, the boat didn't work so we were tourists in the pickup around the towns in the area. We even went riding in a chariot pulled by Clydesdale.

Manitoba, Canada

We flew from Portland to Seattle, Seattle to Vancouver, from Vancouver to Winnipeg, Manitoba. Then it took a couple of more airplanes to get up to Kississing Lake. We stayed there for a week. It was their first season opening after COVID, so the camp was in bad shape, poor maintenance and repair. But we caught lots and lots of pike and mackinaw, or lake trout.

There's lakes up there you can't imagine. One day we fished from the base camp. The next day they'd fly us in a float plane to another lake, then the next day we'd go to still another lake. One day we caught two-hundred fish but we didn't bring any home. The skiffs were about 16′ or 18′ long.

One thing that I thought was interesting, there was a lady that was supposed to be the chef in the kitchen couldn't be there, somebody else was doing it and the food was terrible. I asked for bacon and it was burnt. Then we'd go out fishing. The first two or three fish we'd catch, the skipper would save them. It was about 11:30AM or 12PM, he had a place he'd land the skiff up on the beach. He brought a little stove. It had a propane burner that he'd put two open cans of vegetables on. After he'd filet the fish we caught, he'd smother them with cracker crumbs, and put them in the cast iron skillet. He'd also cut up a bunch of potatoes for French fries. That was the best meal we had all the time we were there.

The temperature was great. We didn't have any mosquitoes. It was all water, so there wasn't any room for them.

Manitoba is such an interesting place. This lake where the lodge was, when you're in a float plane and you're up about 200′, everywhere you look there's lakes. There's a little bit of land here and there, but pretty much water. The lakes are joined together. Some of them you may not see a stream between but underground they're connected. That whole thing is just a swamp. They'll never get fished out. They'll get overpopulated if anything.

Mozambique, Africa

September Andy and I flew to Africa for a safari hunt and Tiger fishing, this is a fish not an animal.

We bought our tickets ahead of time and first class because it's so far. On overseas flights you can stretch out full length. Then even give you pajamas and all that stuff. Lots of personal service.

We had the weapons inspected in Portland and Security sealed the box that they were in. But when we got to Seattle they didn't tell us that we were supposed to have Qatar Airways inspect them again. When it came time to load the plane, the weapons weren't cleared, so we couldn't go. We had reservations to go to an underground diamond mind when we got to Johannesburg, but we didn't get to do that.

It's seventeen-hours flying time. We got to Qatar and had a few hours there. Qatar is a very rich country. They have the biggest gas fields in the world, or so they say. So everything is top, top, top cabin at the mall in the airport. We had another flight to Johannesburg which was eight hours or so. We got to Johannesburg about six o'clock in the morning. We slept in that day, then did a little bit of close quarters sightseeing around the hotel area.

The next morning we went to the airport and met the guide, there were two of them. They were kind of incorporated, one owned the lodge and the other was a guide. We flew north to Mozambique, in South Africa. It was a couple of hour flight. We landed in a town called Tete, where we cleared customs for Mozambique. It took about six or seven hours for them to do nothing. They're not in a hurry about anything. That was about noon. Then we got into pickup and drove about another six hours. By then it's getting almost dark. We stopped at one of the guys lodge, it was up on a mountain.

They drove us up the hill to the mountain top where the lodge was. They have free toddies and all that stuff. They fed us, but I didn't know what it was. I ate everything they put out. They had a little fish that was only about two-inches long. They fix it two different ways. It was like a little tiny herring, some eat it raw and some put seasoning on it, those were appetizers. This was a nice lodge, it had solid walls and all that stuff.

Down below us was the reservoir Lake Cahora Bassa created by the Cahora Bassa dam on the Zambezi river that makes Victoria Falls. It's huge, it's like two-hundred miles long and in some places two or three miles across. Of course the area is mountainous.

The next day, we were on the boat about a twenty-two foot. Here we had two Natives, the two guides, and us. We go another two hours to the next lodge. Here there where thatch-roofed huts that we slept in while we were there. They had cut the palms off palm trees, that was the roof and the sides. The beds were hung from the ceiling, anchored with a line so it didn't swing around, with mosquito net around them. Each of us had one of those little huts. It had a flush toilet and shower. But to get hot water, they had to collect wood then build a fire under the water heater in the yard and pipe to all the places. This took a while to get hot. There was a place where they built a fire and we sat around in lawn chairs socializing and had drinks, then they brought us dinner.

Andy and one guide were hunting for hippopotamus and crocodile. We go into a cove. Andy and the guide climbed up on the hill and hid behind some bushes. After a while, a crocodile came out of the water. They would come out in the daytime especially in the afternoon because the sand gets hot and they like to just lie there in the sand. This crocodile crawled out of the water, but he was only about half. Finally they decided he was just going stay there and sleep awhile. So they shot him. They weren't sure they killed him but he didn't leave.

While they were doing that, we went off into another cove tiger fishing. Tiger fish aren't very big, but they have really long teeth and they are fun to catch. We heard the shots so we knew we better go back. On the shore, there were these Native people running towards the shots too. Because that's how they get their meat. They are not allowed to have a gun. They couldn't buy a weapon or ammunition. All they have is the knife that's homemade They basically have no money.

Andy and the guide were coming down off the hill. They're about 50' away. They weren't sure the crocodile was dead, so they shot him again in the head. He didn't move. They went up and poked him to make sure he's dead. The two Native guys on the boat with us, they jumped down and took a bunch of line and tied the crocodiles mouth shut and lashed him to the boat so they can tow him about a quarter of a mile to a level beach. So the next half hour or hour there were 'atta boys' and congratulations. They measured him and took pictures and all that stuff.

In the meantime, there were about ten or fifteen African natives standing around and they were eager to help they. I think it's a fun thing for them. The Natives helped them slide the crocodile on the boat. His head was up on the cabin and his tail barely missed the water. It's about twenty miles to the camp.

By then, these were different Natives, they were circling around. They helped get the crocodile off the boat. They have to drag it from the boat to a hoist. They had a 4x4 vehicle ATV, only two-wheel drive. I don't know if it was a two-wheel drive or two of the wheels didn't work. Anyway, it wouldn't pull the crocodile. All those Natives had to get around and drag him up the beach. There was a block-and-tackle and hung him up. He was 16′ 4″ long. Andy and I stood there by him. Everybody got more pictures. Then they let him down and drag him over to a sand slab with a post and roof over it. Here's where they're going to butcher him. We went to the lodge to have drinks. The Natives butchered that crocodile out because they were going to get the meat.

The next morning, they got the carcass or what's left of it, it still had the guts in it so it would stink pretty bad unless you did something with it. They drug him down to the shore, tied a line on him and drug him across the bay on another beach. When they open him up, there's a big ball of fishnet.

The Natives make their boats. First of all, they cut a tree down about a foot and a half diameter. They have a handmade hasp and chisel it out inside. It's kind of like a dugout. The natives take the boat and net out, and to make the net sink, they tie rocks on it to hold it down. They use water bottles and cans with lids so it will float on top of the water. They don't buy anything. The net is like a gill net. They put the nets out in the water and the fish get caught and they gather them up. Back home, they clean them out and hang them up to dry. They don't sell that many fish because that's what they live on too. The fish buyer comes around and they get a little bit of money that way. They might buy some cloth or something to make clothes with. They can't buy clothes they make them. Anyway, there's that net, the crocodiles were getting the fish out of the net. When they couldn't get them out, they'd just eat the net. It was just a big ball.

Then Andy went out hippo hunting. I didn't go with them I wasn't feeling well. The guides know where the hippos hang out. Just about every nook and cranny on the river has Natives living there. They catch stuff and live out of the jungle for whatever they can kill. So we stopped at every one of those places. The guides can speak their language, and we find out if there's any hippos around. Then they go looking for them.

They found one that had an active hippo. The hippopotamus lives in the water and they have to put their nose up once in a while to breathe. You only see them but just for a little bit and then they're down again. About an hour before dark they start staying up longer because they're waking up. These coves that they live in, there's some reasonably flat ground. The hippos are vegetarians, so they come out and graze all night.

Andy went up with the guide on a hill to wait. You have to shoot them between their eyes and their ears, because that's where their brain is. When they shoot them they sink, but after a little bit they start building gas inside and they float back up. The Natives comes swarming in the water and drag him ashore. They spent all night skinning and quartering that hippo and cutting it into pieces. There was already a group of Natives that came in their dugouts. The last thing they put on the boat is the hippos hide. They drag the hide up on the bank, it's not real steep. Then they carry the pieces up and put them on the hide.

When they get the pieces up there, there's a whole tribe of Natives standing room with a bag in this hand and a knife in that one. As soon as they get their bag full, they move out some more move in. Not an ounce of meat is wasted. That's a big heyday for them.

2023 - Horror in Alaska

We flew to Ketchikan in August. I was planning on this trip more than anything in my life. I was so happy to get to go do that. I knew the fishing was going to be good and I wanted to show Andy that other people knew about good fishing trips too. We got to Ketchikan and stayed with granddaughter Trina and her husband Mike. We took them up to Salmon Falls to have dinner, it's one of the nicer places out past Clover Pass.

The next morning we were going to go down and catch the ferry but that's when I fell. The rock had a sharp point and that's where I hit my head. It knocked me out, but I was still operating and I don't understand that. I remember getting up and we started walking down to get in the car to go to the docks. The next thing I remember, we were docked in Hollis looking for Kathy Z., who was going to come pick us up. She did and we got our bags.

Out in the bay, I showed Andy where we went crabbing as we went past. When we crossed the Harris river that runs into the bay, the salmon run up there to spawn. Lots of times you go by and see bears fishing. I asked Kathy to stop on the bridge, which is not a good idea but there's not a lot of traffic in that country. But there wasn't a bear there.

I don't remember anything else until the next day I guess. We went out to Fireweed Lodge, because we could use of one of their vehicles. I wanted to go to Thorne Bay so I could show Andy where we started the gas company. I was planning on seeing a friend, Longbow, but couldn't get a hold of him.

There's a little bit about driving over I remember. In Thorne Bay nothing looked familiar to me, which was weird. This one place, Bo wanted to buy it. We were going to pay for it but control the operation. It was an auction by telephone. When it got up to $5,000, I quit bidding. Bobbie and Bo were all upset with me because I wouldn't agree to spend any more money. Well, we'd already taken a quick lash and lost $100,000 or so. Anyway, that's just history.

I remember we got a sandwich there and a Coke, ate that, drove around where the grocery store was and went back to the Fireweed Lodge. I met Chase, Bob A.'s wife. We went back to Kathy's but I don't remember any of that. We spent the night there. We stopped and saw Jerry Z. and his wife. I remember standing in their living room, and I remember about thirty seconds and that's all I remember. Then we went out and got in the pickup and drove off.

The next morning we went down and got on the boat. Andy said it took a while, so we must have gone to the outside water before we started fishing. The next thing I knew I was in Seattle, looking at Anne and Kathy, and Ed and Jan.

Andy said I started vomiting, so he called 911. They had an ambulance come up from Klawock, but in the meantime they called an air medevac out of Ketchikan. They put me on the plane out of Klawock and I got flown to Seattle. From there, took me by ambulance to the Hospital.

The Hospital had called them and told them I was there. They said they were going to have to do surgery and they didn't know if I'd make it or not. It was three o'clock in the morning when Anne got the call. She called Kathy and came up that morning. They also called Ed and Jan. Anne's grandson worked in Seattle, so he was there too.

Anyway, I woke up and there were different people there. I was just coming in and out of it for a few days. I really was lucky to live.

I was in the hospital about two weeks. The first several days I didn't know anything. After they did surgery, it was in and out. After I had been there about two and a half weeks, they had the ambulance pick me up and sent me to Woodburn, Oregon to rehab. Woodburn is just a few miles from us in Canby. I was in Woodburn for about another two and a half weeks.

There, they exercised me every day. I had to be able to get in and out of a car before they'd let me leave. So I'd go and walk in the yard, and then they'd have me get in and out of the car a couple of times. Finally they let me go home. Anne came and got me. The Rehab came out an inspected the house to make sure it had grabbed bars and that kind of stuff. They came every day for a while. That was probably another couple of weeks.

I had forty-eight staples in my head. There was a bunch of them. It was at least a ten-inch gash. They folded the crown back and cleaned up the brain blood and put it back down. I didn't know they could do stuff like that.

After my fall, my brain became kind of slow. But eventually the thought would come around. It's kind of surprising, I'll put in a request and pretty soon it comes out.

2024 – Here I Sit

Was mainly spent in Canby, just sitting right here in my chair.

My Philosophy

They're letting all these young people come in the country. They've got to be some terrorists, I just know. I'm so positive I'd give you 100-to-1 odds that they're going to start tearing our country apart if Trump doesn't get elected.

I'm not sure where this country's going. I won't live long enough to see the results, but it's going to happen sooner or later.

I keep looking back, when you look back to the 1900s where the country was, even further back than that, it keeps gradually getting worse. It's getting so bad now, I keep telling myself God's in control. Now where he's going to take us I don't know. He knows how it's going to end, because he created the world and everything in it.

Another thing I cannot understand is an atheist's mind. I can't imagine anybody can't believe the world can turn a certain speed and not vary more than a second, and tilt at an angle so the seasons come at the same time. It's a simple little thing for God.

A lot of things I think about. The earth is one, because at the center of the earth is this kind of material and then there us another layer of something else, and then another. God put oil, gas, and coal in the ground for us to find. All those planets and stars in the sky. I can't imagine anybody not understanding that this didn't just happen. I came to believe, because my parents and grandparents were all religious people. I think about all these things. The stars. The sun is 93-million miles away and it's heating us down here. Many things like that. There's no explanation for it other than God created it.

Male and female create babies. When Jesus was created I don't know if he came down and did Mary, but it was God's child that came out of there. You think about your body, you put stuff in your body and it goes in your stomach. It kind of dissolves and goes off in the little intestine, and then it distributes it throughout your body, then the big intestine and the big boom at the end.

It's all so huge. I can't imagine anybody not believing in God. I can't believe they're even qualified to breathe even.

Now I'm in the Twilight of My Years

Mom used to say she was glad I was so inquisitive, because that's how you learn stuff. My Uncle, who stayed with us when I was just a little kid, he used to pay me money, like a dime once in a while, for *not* asking him questions. I had to know about everything. I see little kids like that now and I can see it's irritating. "What's that?" "How does that work?" But I've always been inquisitive about things. That's why I've always been doing different stuff. I wasn't satisfied with routine, I wanted something different. I've always been like that.

I wouldn't give you a wooden nickel worth for anymore, but I wouldn't take $1,000,000 for the memories that I've got.

God has blessed me and Anne many times. Because if it hadn't been for Him, I'm sure I wouldn't be here.

In fact, He's blessed me most all my life.

Frank Permenter

www.ingramcontent.com/pod-product-compliance
Lightning Source LLC
Chambersburg PA
CBHW031515040426
42445CB00009B/233